ACKEE AND PLANTAIN

Contemporary Vegan Caribbean Recipes by RGVEGAN

First published 2022 by **RGVEGAN**

A CIP catalogue record for this title is available from the British Library.

ISBN: 9781739861841

RGVEGAN
www.rgvegan.co.uk
ramoan@rgvegan.co.uk

Food photography:	Ramoan Gunter
Graphic Designer:	barbaraborko.com
Portrait Photography:	Jake Green
Copyeditor:	Charlotte Thompson

All materials are sourced from sustainably managed forests.

FRIED DUMPLING TOPPED WITH AVOCADO MASH, FRIED PLANTAIN & ACKEE

CONTENTS

MY FOOD STORY

Growing up, the flavours, tastes and scents of Caribbean food always got my taste buds going. Aromas of ginger, nutmeg, coconut, Scotch bonnet pepper, thyme, cinnamon, allspice - even now I can still smell the warm, tantalising flavours of my nan's cooking bubbling, simmering and sizzling away on the hob.

Rice and peas, plantain, soups, ackee, callaloo, dumplings - the list goes on. Foods which ignited memories of home for my grandparents are visions of distant shores for me. As a child of Jamaican descent, the Caribbean isles were always a part of my present - an underlying thread of history which remains a distinct component of the pulse of who I am.

Caribbean food is a large element of my strong sense of identity – a sensory connection which never fades so those flavours and tastes stayed with me.

As I got older, the diversity and moreishness of those belly-filling meals were always at the heart of what I craved. Over the years, other cuisines and tastes would come and go, but it was always Caribbean cooking that I came back to.

I was lucky to grow up watching and learning from my nan as she cooked, absorbing the sleight of hand, secret tweaks and combinations of spices which made her food taste so good. As I moved closer towards a vegan-led diet, I began to truly appreciate the depth of choice Caribbean food offered.

COOKING RG STYLE

My recipes are inspired by the tastes and flavours of Caribbean cuisine.

Although my own heritage is Jamaican, the inspiration for my recipes comes from all over the Caribbean.

With a history which spans many continents and cooking styles, Caribbean meals are a diverse, rich fusion of foods and flavours from around the world, including Africa, India, France and Spain.

Each Caribbean island has its own signature dishes, cultural influences and individual ways of spicing, cooking and combining ingredients. However, across the islands, meals retain a distinct familiarity which marks them out as Caribbean cooking – lip-smacking, flavourful dishes packed with familiar fresh vegetables, fruits, herbs and spices.

USING THESE RECIPES

The meals in this book are dishes I enjoy eating on a daily basis. None of the ingredients are too expensive or hard to find. Use my list of cupboard essentials and hacks to check you have all you need whilst learning more about where to source your Caribbean staples.

Caribbean cooking is about passion and taste. Like many other global cuisines, this style of cooking is not about recipes which need to be followed word for word.

Caribbean foods are mouthwatering, hearty meals passed down through families from one generation to another, with many tweaks and adjustments along the way.

In the same spirit, the recipes in this book are delicious, satisfying meals bursting with flavours, herbs and spices - ready for you to make your own. Switch things up and swap things in to suit your personal taste.

I cook Caribbean-inspired vegan food so all the recipes in this book are vegan. If you look at the heritage of Jamaica alone, it's easy to see, vegan meals and Caribbean cooking go hand in hand.

The Caribbean hosts a wealth of ital food - fresh fruits, vegetables, spices and herbs. All of which can be found growing wild in back gardens and along roadsides. Vegan cooking has long been apart of the fabric of Caribbean cuisine.

For me, eating a plant-based diet is a choice. You'll find my recipes are packed with flavour, colour, variety and taste. I largely use whole foods and steer clear of meat replicas however the options for you are open. If there are dietary or lifestyle requirements which mean you want to use alternative ingredients, I encourage you to do so.

Experiment, enjoy the process, discover your favourite spice combinations and unlock your own Caribbean cooking style.

STORE CUPBOARD ESSENTIALS

ACKEE

Soft and easy to cook, ackee is a delicious, signature ingredient in Jamaican cookery. Used throughout the Caribbean, ackee has a striking red skin and a soft yellow flesh with black seeds at its centre. The flesh is the only part that is eaten. Unripe ackee contains a deadly poison called hypoglycin so it can only be picked when the fruit's protective pods turn red and open naturally.

Ackee and saltfish is the national dish of Jamaica. The delicate yellow flesh can be paired with just about anything and in the UK you'll find it ready to use in a tin.

ALLSPICE

Spicy, peppery and fragrant, allspice is an important staple in any Caribbean kitchen.

Used widely throughout the Caribbean, allspice is derived from the dried berries of the pimento tree. You can find both ground and whole allspice berries in the seasoning aisle in most supermarkets.

Allspice is a key ingredient in jerk seasoning however it does have a powerful flavour so should be used liberally.

BREADFRUIT

The white, soft and starchy flesh of breadfruit has long been favoured across the Caribbean. Easy to grow and used in a vast range of ways, breadfruit is predicted to become a global superfood in the near future.

Packed with an abundance of vitamins and minerals, this tasty, gluten-free carbohydrate can be boiled, grilled, fried, steamed, ground into flour and more.

High in beneficial amino acids, the subtle flavour of breadfruit means it can be used in any dish as a healthier alternative to carbohydrates, such as potatoes or rice.

CHO CHO

Part of the squash family, cho cho (also known as chayote & christophine) is similar to an apple in texture. Light in flavour with a green skin, cho cho is low in calories, packed with antioxidants and easy to use.

Like other squashes, cho cho can be boiled, fried, baked, mashed or even eaten raw.

CALLALOO

Similar in appearance and texture to spinach or greens but with a more appealing taste, callaloo is a versatile, nutritious leafy vegetable which makes a welcome addition to any meal.

Rich in vitamins, iron and fibre, callaloo can be used in the same way as other leafy greens, in mains,

sides, soups and more. You can find callaloo sold fresh in bunches or chopped in a tin, ready for use.

COCONUT MILK

One of the most recognisable flavours in Caribbean cooking is coconut milk.

Easily added to the pan, coconut milk is the most convenient way to impart the irresistibly nutty taste of coconut to any dish. If you are cooking anything, particularly rice and peas or curries, coconut milk will add a delicious, velvety smooth finish.

COCONUT SUGAR

Obtained from the dried sugary sap of the coconut plant, coconut sugar is a flavoursome natural sweetener, similar to brown sugar. You can buy it from Caribbean food shops and health food stores.

CREAMED COCONUT

Smooth coconut cream delivers a nutty flavour and creamy texture. Not to be confused with coconut milk, coconut cream is sold in a convenient block so you can cut off small chunks and store the rest in the fridge.

More suitable to use for multiple meals than coconut milk, coconut cream adds a delicious taste and finish to many dishes, including rice and peas.

GREEN BANANA

Green bananas have a delicate flavour which makes them a perfect substitute for potatoes and yams. Ideal for pairing with sauces and soups, green bananas are a tasty, nutritious and versatile ingredient.

Green bananas are inexpensive and filling. They are often displayed next to plantain or yams. Green bananas have a firm green skin and a dense texture.

Green bananas should only be eaten when cooked and the skin discarded. It is best to boil green bananas in their skin for easy removal after. Rinse the skin with salty water before boiling.

COCONUT OIL

You can find coconut oil just about anywhere these days. It is usually solid when bought but will melt into a liquid when heated. The flavour is unbeatable and you can even make your own coconut oil from scratch.

CORNMEAL

Cornmeal is a much- loved staple across the Caribbean and can be used like oats or flour to make everything from porridge to bread, puddings, dumplings and more.

Made from ground maize, the irresistible texture, flavour and versatility of cornmeal makes it a popular comfort food which instantly transports you back home.

Gluten-free and rich in vitamins and minerals, cornmeal is guaranteed to leave you feeling warm, nourished and satisfied.

THYME

Fresh thyme is a major flavour in Caribbean cooking. It has a wonderful, complex taste that is completely different to the dried thyme commonly sold in UK supermarkets. You could even grow your own supply of fresh thyme in a pot at home.

Bunches of fresh thyme can be easily found in any Caribbean food shop. Store sprigs of fresh thyme in a cup on the kitchen window sill or loosely wrapped in kitchen towel in the fridge.

WHERE TO SHOP

The range of ingredients on sale in our supermarkets seems to get more diverse with each visit. Many top supermarkets have been at the forefront of stocking Caribbean ingredients in increasing quantities. However, the variety and quality of Caribbean foods on sale in UK supermarkets is still small and largely overpriced.

Instead, head to Asian, African and Caribbean food shops and market stalls to uncover a treasure trove of exciting, fresh ingredients plus canned goods and dried products - all at low or relatively cheap prices.

If you're not sure where to find your local Asian, African or Caribbean food store, talk to colleagues and friends who will willingly share their favourite finds whilst giving some great tips on what they like to buy there!

Many people are willing to cross boroughs and counties to locate the best ingredients so it's always worth asking around to discover hidden gems.

Look out for top brands such as Dunn's River, Grace and Walkerswood when buying tinned or packaged foods.

RECIPES

FRIED PLANTAIN

INGREDIENTS

1-2 servings

1 large plantain
1 tbsp coconut oil
sea salt

METHOD

1 Heat a frying pan on a medium heat with enough coconut oil to coat the surface generously.

2 Cut the ends off the plantain and slit lengthways.

3 Remove the plantain skin.

4 Slice approximately ½ cm slices at an angle.

5 Place plantain into hot frying and fry on each side for 1-2 minutes until golden.

6 Place the cooked pieces of plantain on the paper towel to soak up any excess oil and then you're ready to eat.

Optional: sprinkle with a little salt to taste.

smeg

RED PEA STEW & SPINNERS

INGREDIENTS

4 servings

2 cups kidney beans, dried
6 cups water
6 garlic cloves
1 onion
2 spring onions
1 carrot
½ red pepper
½ green pepper
1 Scotch bonnet pepper
6 or 8 sprigs of fresh thyme
1½ tbsp sea salt
coconut milk (400ml)

Spinners

½ cup plain flour
¼ water
½ tsp salt
½ tsp allspice (optional)

METHOD

1 Wash the dried kidney beans and leave them to soak in fresh water overnight.

2 The next day, rinse the kidney beans again before placing in a saucepan with water. Add the sea salt, top with a lid left slightly open and bring to a low boil until the beans are soft.

3 Chop the garlic, onions, spring onions, carrot and red pepper then place them into the pan of softened beans. Next pour in the coconut milk followed by the thyme and the whole scotch bonnet pepper, pierced at one end.

Stir everything together, top with the lid and leave to cook on a gentle simmer.

4 In a bowl, mix together the flour, salt and allspice. Add the water and mix well to form a dough. Break off a thumb- sized piece of the dough, place it between your hands and rub your hands together (as if you are trying to keep your hands warm) to form a long thin shape. Repeat until all the spinners are made then add them to the boiling bean mixture.

5 Simmer for a final 25-30 minutes. The stew will begin to thicken and continue to thicken as it cools. Remove the Scotch bonnet pepper and leave to cool before serving.

RICE & PEAS

INGREDIENTS

Approx 6 servings

2 cups basmati or long grain rice
1 cup kidney beans, dried
5 thyme sprigs
2 spring onions
1 onion
1 tsp jerk seasoning paste
1 Scotch bonnet pepper
1 tsp allspice
4 garlic cloves
1 or 2 tsp sea salt
coconut milk (400ml)

METHOD

1 Rinse the kidney beans and leave them to soak in fresh water overnight.

2 The next day, rinse the beans again before placing in a saucepan with water. Top the pan with a lid left slightly open then boil the beans so the water is bubbling for 45 minutes - 1 hour, until the beans are soft.

3 Once the beans have begun to soften, add minced garlic plus finely chopped onion and spring onions followed by the thyme, coconut milk, allspice, whole Scotch bonnet pepper and salt. Mix together and leave to cook on a medium heat for 30 minutes with the lid on.

4 Rinse the rice in a bowl of water 3-4 times until the water begins to look clear. Drain the rice then add to the saucepan of beans and mix together. Check the water level is an inch higher than the rice, if it isn't, add more water.

5 Leave the rice to cook. When it begins to boil, turn the heat down to a low setting and simmer with the lid on for 20 minutes. Halfway through, gently stir the rice, lifting it up from the bottom of the pan with a fork.

6 After 20 minutes, turn the heat off, stir again with a fork and leave to cool slightly, topped with a lid, before serving.

PLANTAIN & LENTIL STEW

INGREDIENTS

4-6 servings

2 onions
6 garlic cloves
2 carrots
1 bell pepper
2 tomatoes
½ tsp jerk paste
2 tbsp corn flour
2 plantains
2 or 3 sprigs of thyme
1 tbsp herbes de Provence
green lentils, cooked (300g)
chestnut mushrooms (500g)
vegetable stock (300ml)
coconut oil
sea salt
black pepper
vegan Worcestershire sauce

METHOD

1 Heat some oil in a pan. Add chopped garlic, onions, carrots and bell pepper followed by the thyme, herbes de Provence, salt and black pepper.

2 After 10 minutes, stir in chopped mushrooms and tomatoes, a splash of Worcestershire sauce and the jerk paste. Leave to cook on a medium heat until the mushrooms are cooked.

3 Next, add the cooked green lentils and vegetable stock to the pan. Mix 2 tbsp of corn flour with 200ml of cold water and stir it into the pan. Leave to cook on a low - medium heat for 15 minutes, stirring regularly until the mixture begins to thicken.

4 Peel, cut and fry the plantain then add it to the stew. Leave the stew to cook, topped with a lid, for a further 5 minutes.

After 5 minutes, turn off the heat and allow the stew to cool slightly before serving.

ITAL LENTIL & BEAN COCONUT CURRY

INGREDIENTS

6 servings

1 large onion
1 tbsp cumin seeds
1 red bell pepper
4 spring onions
1 carrots
2 tomatoes
1 piece of fresh ginger
2 tbsp curry powder
1 tbsp tomato puree
1 tbsp coconut sugar
8 sprigs of fresh thyme
1 cup vegetable stock
1 Scotch bonnet pepper
10 garlic cloves
coconut milk (400ml)
creamed coconut (50g)
green lentils, cooked (230g)
kidney beans, cooked (230g)
fresh callaloo (50g), chopped (optional)
sea salt
black pepper

METHOD

1 Heat a little oil in a large, deep saucepan. Add chopped onions and garlic plus cumin seeds then cook until the onions become translucent.

2 Chop the red pepper, springs onions, carrots, tomatoes and ginger then stir into the pan followed by the curry powder, tomato puree, coconut sugar, fresh thyme and sea salt.

3 Mix together for 2-3 minutes before pouring in the coconut milk, creamed coconut, vegetable stock, green lentils, kidney beans and whole Scotch bonnet pepper, pierced at one end.

4 Leave to cook on a medium heat with the lid on for 30 minutes, stirring regularly.

5 Towards the end of cooking, you can add the optional callaloo if you wish. Allow to cool slightly before serving.

PLANTAIN WAFFLES

INGREDIENTS

Makes 8 quarters

1 ripe plantain
1½ tsp baking powder
1 tsp cinnamon
2 tbsp orange extract
white spelt flour (60g)
oat milk (100ml)
extra virgin olive oil (50ml)

METHOD

1. First peel and chop the plantain into small pieces before adding to a large bowl (this will make the plantain a little easier to mash).
2. Mash the plantain as much as you can then add flour, baking powder, cinnamon and salt. Mix together until all the ingredients are combined.
3. Next, stir in the nut milk until a pancake-like batter is formed then add olive oil and orange extract and mix well.
4. Pour the mixture into a waffle iron and cook until golden brown.

MIXED PEPPER QUINOA

Quinoa can be quite bland on its own so this recipe is the perfect way to infuse a little flavour. You can be quite creative with this one and swap my suggestions for your favourite herbs and spices.

INGREDIENTS

6-8 servings

3 Bell peppers
1 onion
4 garlic cloves
5 tbsp balsamic vinegar
coconut oil
quinoa (300g)
sea salt
black pepper

METHOD

1. Ideally, the quinoa should be left to soak in water overnight. However, if you don't have time, soak the quinoa for at least 2 hours to ensure it has a lovely, soft consistency when cooked.

2. Rinse the soaked quinoa and place it in a saucepan. Top with fresh water, stopping ½ cm above the quinoa. Season with a pinch of salt then cook on a medium heat until the water begins to boil.

3. Turn the heat to low, top with a lid and leave to simmer for up to 10 minutes (if you didn't soak the quinoa overnight it may take a bit longer).

4. When the quinoa is soft and fluffy, take it off the heat, run a fork through the grains to aid cooling then leave to cool with the lid off.

5. Finely dice the bell peppers (I tend to use one of each colour). Heat a little oil in a large saucepan or wok. Add chopped onion and garlic plus the peppers to the pan then mix together on a high heat to dry out the peppers.

6. Once the peppers have reduced, pour the quinoa into the pan and mix well. Season with the balsamic vinegar, salt and pepper to finish.

ACKEE & KALAMATA OLIVES

This is another of my favourite ackee combinations.
The saltiness of the olives is reminiscent of the salted cod in the original Jamaican recipe, delivering a similar satisfying taste.
I've tried this recipe with a number of different type of olives and have found Kalamata olives that work best.

INGREDIENTS

4 servings

1 onion
4 garlic cloves
1 tsp fresh thyme
2 red pointed peppers
1 tomato
½ Scotch bonnet pepper, deseeded (optional)
1 tsp cayenne pepper
10 to 12 kalamata olives
ackee, tinned (540g)
coconut oil

Ackee and kalamata olives with: baked beans, curry mushrooms, buttered cabbage, mixed pepper quinoa, fried plantain and avocado hummus.

METHOD

1 Heat a little oil in a frying pan over a medium heat. Add chopped onion, garlic and the thyme. Sauté for 2-3 minutes then add choppedpeppers, tomato, cayenne pepper followed by the optional Scotch bonnet pepper, chopped fine.

I've removed the seeds from the Scotch bonnet pepper on this occasion.

Cook on a low - medium heat for 8 minutes.

2 Gently drain and rinse the ackee in a large strainer or colander then add to the pan followed by chopped kalamata olives. Carefully mix everything together so the ackee does not get crushed. Add a splash of water, put the lid on the pan and leave on a low heat for 5 minutes.

3 Season with salt and pepper then leave to cool slightly before serving.

ROASTED ACKEE

Roasted ackee with king oyster mushroom strips cooked in butter, grilled tomatoes, smoked hummus, fried plantain, a BBQ burger, sauteed tenderstem broccoli, avocado and baked beans.

INGREDIENTS

2 - 4 servings

1 tbsp dried thyme
sea salt
ackee, tinned (540g)
extra virgin olive oil
black pepper

METHOD

1 Gently rinse and drain the ackee then place in a large bowl.

2 Drizzle the ackee with extra virgin olive oil and season with the dried thyme, black pepper and sea salt.

3 Gently toss the bowl or carefully mix the ingredients until thoroughly covered (avoid harsh stirring which will crush the ackee).

4 Line a baking tray with greaseproof paper and use a light touch to spread the seasoned ackee evenly across the tray.

5 Place in a preheated oven at 200°c for 15 - 20 minutes, removing when the ackee begins to slightly change colour and take on a firmer texture.

SWEET POTATO PIZZA BASE

INGREDIENTS

Medium sized base

- 2 tbsp herbes de Provence
- 1 tbsp tomato powder
- ½ tsp sea salt black pepper
- 1 tsp garlic powder
- ½ tsp jerk seasoning
- 1 tsp baking powder
- ¼ cup extra virgin olive oil
- white spelt flour (70g)
- sweet potato (350g)

METHOD

1. Peel and cut your potatoes into small cubes. Place in a steamer and steam until soft.

2. Drain off as much excess water as possible and leave to cool for 5 minutes. When the time is up, place the potatoes in a large bowl and mash with the back of a fork until smooth.

3. Add the herbes de Provence, tomato powder, sea salt, black pepper, garlic powder, jerk seasoning, baking powder and olive oil to the mashed potato and mix together well. Sieve the flour into the mash then combine the ingredients together until a dough is formed.

4. Cover the dough with damp kitchen towel and leave it in the fridge for 10 minutes.

5. Remove the dough from the fridge and place it in the centre of a pizza tray lined with non- stick parchment paper. Gently press the dough out into a rough circle with your fingers to form an even pizza base. Pierce the surface of the pizza base with a fork several times.

6. Cook in a preheated oven at 190°C for about 30 minutes, removing once the surface starts to turn golden brown. Cover the pizza with the topping of your choice. I used a tomato and herb jerk bqq sauce topped with a mixture of ackee, onions, garlic, peppers, fried mushrooms, fried plantain & sun-dried tomatoes.

SCOTCH BONNET HUMMUS

Scotch bonnet hummus on toasted sourdough topped with avocado, fried plantain, tomatoes, spring onions and toasted sesame seeds.

INGREDIENTS

4 servings

2 tbsp tahini
2 garlic cloves
1 lemon, juiced
½ Scotch bonnet pepper
½ tsp paprika
1 tsp salt
cashew nuts (50g) (optional)
chickpeas (400g)
extra virgin olive oil (180ml)
water (100ml)

METHOD

1. Place the chickpeas in cold water and gently rub the outsides to remove the skin.

2. Once the skins are removed, put the chickpeas, tahini, garlic, lemon juice, Scotch bonnet pepper, cashew nuts, paprika, water and salt into a high speed blender or food processor.

3. With the machine running, slowly add the olive oil to the mixture through the top of the blender, until the hummus is smooth. If the mixture is too thick, keep adding water until the hummus has the consistency you desire.

CREAMY ACKEE SCOTCH BONNET PASTA

30 min - 45 min

INGREDIENTS

4 - 6 servings

2 onions
5 garlic cloves
4 large tomatoes
2 tbsp herbes de Provence
2 tbsp grated vegan parmesan
½ Scotch bonnet pepper
1 courgette
3 nori sheets
4 sprigs of fresh thyme
2 or 3 tbsp fresh dill
coconut milk (400ml)
sun-dried tomatoes (100g)
ackee, tinned (540g)
thumb-sized piece of ginger
sea salt
lack pepper
cashew nuts (optional) (50g)

METHOD

1 Heat a drizzle of olive in a pan on a low to medium heat. Add chopped onions, garlic, ginger and cashew nuts plus herbes de Provence and the Scotch bonnet pepper. Sauté for 5 minutes before adding the chopped tomatoes. Cook for a further 6 minutes until the tomatoes begin to break down.

2 Transfer the cooked ingredients into a blender add the coconut milk and blend until smooth.

3 Pour the blended sauce back into the saucepan on a low to medium heat. Stir in the thyme, sliced courgette, chopped sun-dried tomatoes, grated parmesan and torn nori sheets. Season with salt and black pepper then reduce the heat and simmer for 10 minutes, stirring occasionally.

4 Turn off the heat and gently fold in the drained and rinsed ackee plus chopped dill.

5 Top with fried courgette pieces, sautéed ackee, chopped sun-dried tomatoes and toasted pine nuts. Serve alongside penne pasta in a green pesto sauce with fresh dill.

SAVOURY CREAM OF RICE

Cream of rice makes a delicious alternative to porridge and is also a great post-workout snack. It is fat-free, sodium-free and gluten-free.

INGREDIENTS

2 servings

½ cup cream of rice
2 cups water
3 garlic cloves
½ an onion
1 tsp dairy-free butter
pinch of salt
black pepper

METHOD

1 Heat the butter. Add finely chopped onions and garlic then sauté for a few minutes until soft.

2 Next, place the water, sea salt and cream of rice in the pan then whisk everything together. Continue to whisk gently on a medium heat until the mixture begins to thicken.

3 Season with pepper before serving.

Savoury cream of rice topped with sautéed asparagus, fried plantain mushrooms, tomatoes, pine nuts, red pepper and spring onion.

NO BEEF BURGER

You can also use this recipe to make 'no meat' meatballs.
The mixture can be frozen for use at a later date.

INGREDIENTS

Makes 6 burgers

5 garlic cloves
1 onion
½ ripe plantain
1 tbsp tomato paste
1 tbsp red onion chutney
½ tsp jerk paste
3 tbsp BBQ sauce
2 tbsp herbes de Provence
1 tbsp coconut oil
mixed beans, tinned (150g)
chickpeas, tinned (150g)
young jackfruit, tinned (250g)
chestnut mushrooms (250g)
grated cheese (optional) (50g)
chickpea flour (150-200g)
pickled beetroot (50g)
sea salt
black pepper

METHOD

1 Slowly sauté the chopped garlic, onions, jackfruit and mushrooms in coconut oil for 15 minutes then leave to one side to cool.

2 Blend the pickled beetroot, ripe plantain, tomato paste, jerk paste, red onion chutney, BBQ sauce, herbes de Provence, sea salt and black pepper to taste plus half of the mixed beans and chickpeas in a food processor.

3 Mash the remaining mixed beans and chickpeas together so they still retain some texture.

4 Place all the sautéed ingredients, blended ingredients and mashed pulses together in a large mixing bowl and combine. Then add the chickpea flour and the optional cheese. The mixture should have the consistency of 'tuna mayo', if it is too runny add more chickpea flour.

5 Line a baking tray with parchment paper and spoon the mixture onto the paper and shape with your hands into burger shapes or with the back of a spoon.

6 Place in a preheated oven at 200°c (fan) for 15 minutes. You can finish with shallow frying the burgers on each side and around the edges to give it a crispy finish for 2- 3 minutes.

No Beef Burger served in a wholewheat bread bun with lettuce, tomatoes, red onion chutney, baby gherkins and fried plantain.

RED LENTIL DAHL

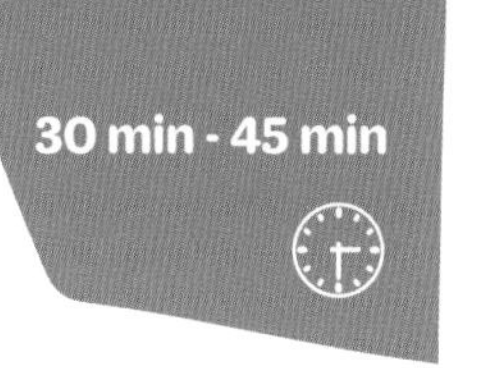

INGREDIENTS

6-8 servings

1 tbsp dairy-free butter
2 onions
6 or 8 garlic cloves
1 tbsp cumin seeds
2 or 3 tomatoes
1 tsp ginger powder
1 tsp salt
1 tsp black pepper
1 or 2 tsp chilli flakes
4 bay leaves
1 cinnamon stick
1 tbsp cinnamon
½ tsp ground turmeric
1 tbsp garam masala
1 tsp tomato paste
red lentils (300g)
coconut milk (300ml)
handful of fresh coriander

Dal served with garlic and herb bread, fried plantain and coconut yoghurt.

METHOD

1. Wash the red lentils thoroughly until the water is clear. Place the lentils in a saucepan and fill with water, stopping 1cm above the lentils then cook on a medium heat.

   When the lentils begin to boil, spoon away the froth at the top. Leave to cook with the lid on for a further 25 minutes until the lentils are soft and mushy. Top up the water when necessary to ensure the lentils don't dry out.

2. Next, add chopped onions and garlic plus cumin seeds to a pan of melted butter then sauté for 5 minutes on a low-medium heat.

3. Chop the tomatoes and add them to the pan along with the cinnamon stick, bay leaves, tomato paste, turmeric, ginger powder, chilli flakes, salt and pepper. Mix together and place on a low - medium heat for 15-20mins until the tomatoes have cooked down and the mixture is almost fully combined.

4. Drain off any water left in the lentils before adding the tomato mixture. Then add coconut milk, chopped coriander, garam masala and cinnamon. Leave on a low heat for 10-15 minutes, mixing throughout. Allow to cool before serving.

ROASTED VEGETABLE PASTA

INGREDIENTS

6 servings

Vegetables

2 bell peppers
1 courgette
1 carrot
½ aubergine
2 tomatoes
1 red onion
chestnut mushrooms (100g)
olive oil
black pepper
sea salt

Sauce

7 garlic cloves
1 large onion
1 tbsp herbes de Provence
1 tbsp oregano
1 tsp smoked paprika
½ cup red wine (or red grape juice)
1 tbsp tomato paste
tomato passata (500g)
splash of balsamic vinegar
black pepper
sea salt
pasta of choice

Roasted vegetable pasta topped with toasted pine nuts and cress.

METHOD

1 Chop and slice the vegetables then place them onto a large baking tray. The vegetables are interchangeable so feel free to swap any listed with those of your choice.

Add a generous drizzle of olive oil plus a sprinkle of salt and black pepper then roast in the oven for 40 mins on 160°c (fan). After 20 minutes, turn the vegetables over then leave to roast for the remaining 20 minutes.

2 Whilst the vegetables roast, heat a large saucepan with coconut oil and add the finely chopped onions, garlic and herbes de Provence. Sauté for 3-4 minutes before pouring in the passata, oregano, smoked paprika, red wine and balsamic vinegar. Season with salt and black pepper then leave to cook on a low - medium heat.

3 Once the vegetables have finished roasting add them to the sauce. Mix together and turn off the heat after 5 minutes.

4 Add your pasta of choice to a pan of boiling water seasoned with a little sea salt. Once the pasta is cooked and drained, stir it into the roasted vegetable sauce.

5 I like to eat mine topped with toasted pine nuts, green pesto and cress.

MUSHROOM & PEPPERCORN SAUCE

INGREDIENTS

4 servings

VEGETABLES

2 shallots (or onions)
4 garlic cloves
1 tbsp dairy-free butter
2 tbsp olive oil
2 to 3 tbsp crushed peppercorns
2 tbsp fresh parsley
mushrooms (500g)
vegetable stock (200ml)
splash of brandy (optional)

CREAM

1 garlic clove
1 tbsp crushed peppercorns
½ lemon, juiced
cashew nuts (150g)
mushrooms, cooked (50g) (from the 500g above)
drizzle of olive oil
water

METHOD

1 Crush peppercorns using a Pestle and mortar or pepper grinder.

2 Finely dice the shallots and garlic then gently cook in heated butter and olive oil along with crushed peppercorns. If you wish, you can add splash of brandy and flambé the sauce to add an extra layer of depth. I'd recommend to watch a flambé tutorial video before doing so, to keep yourself safe if you haven't done it before.

3 Slice the mushrooms and add them to the pan. Once cooked, stir in the vegetable stock and leave to reduce slightly.

4 In the meantime, add all the ingredients for the cashew cream plus roughly 50g of the mushrooms from the pan to a high speed blender. Top with water stopping at the level of the cashew nuts then blend until the mixture has a consistency similar to custard.

5 Pour the cashew cream into the pan and mix with the mushrooms. Stir the sauce for 3-5 minutes until your preferred level of creaminess is achieved, adding more water when necessary. Top with another tablespoon of crushed peppercorns and parsley to finish. Serve with homemade chips, roasted tenderstem broccoli and a seared tomato.

PLANTAIN & KIDNEY BEAN CURRY

INGREDIENTS

4 servings

1 tbsp cumin seeds
1 large onion
5 garlic cloves
2 large tomatoes
3 to 5 bay leaves
2 spring onions
2 to 3 sprigs of thyme
½ Scotch bonnet
1 tbsp curry powder
1 bell pepper
1 tbsp tomato paste
1 tsp ground cinnamon
½ tsp garam masala
½ tsp allspice
2 plantains
kidney beans, cooked (200g)
coconut oil
sea salt
black pepper
cinnamon stick
pepper
coconut milk (200ml)

METHOD

1 Peel, slice and fry the plantains in coconut oil until golden then put to one side.

2 Heat a little coconut oil in a frying pan. Add chopped onions and garlic plus the cumin then sauté for 2-3 minutes. Next stir in chopped tomatoes and spring onion followed by the salt, black pepper, cinnamon stick, bay leaves, thyme, Scotch bonnet pepper, curry powder and a little water.

3 After 5-7 minutes, add the coconut milk followed by chopped bell pepper, cooked kidney beans and the tomato paste. Pour in a little more water then cover the pan with a lid and cook for 25 minutes on a low - medium heat, stirring occasionally.

4 Finally, add the ground cinnamon, garam masala, allspice and cooked plantains. Mix together then turn off the heat after 3 minutes, top with a lid and serve.

NANNY'S ACKEE

INGREDIENTS

4 servings

8 garlic cloves
1 onion
½ red pepper
½ green pepper
2 spring onions
2 to 3 sprigs of thyme
2 tomatoes
2 bay leaves
1 Scotch bonnet
1 tsp allspice
1 tsp sea salt
pepper
coconut oil
ackee (540g)
black pepper

METHOD

1 Heat a little oil in a frying pan. Add chopped onions and garlic plus the thyme. Sauté for 2-3 minutes before adding chopped peppers, spring onions and tomatoes followed by the bay leaves, allspice, salt and black pepper. Pierce a hole in the Scotch bonnet pepper with a knife and add it to the mixture.

2 Sauté for a further 8-10 minutes on a low-medium heat. Gently drain and rinse the ackee in a strainer or colander then add to the pan.

Carefully mix everything together to avoid crushing. Leave to cook for another 5 minutes then turn off the heat and season with salt and pepper.

3 Remove the Scotch bonnet pepper before serving.

Nanny's Ackee served with fried plantain, fried dumplings, sweetcorn, yam, green banana, pumpkin, chayote and coleslaw.

FRAGRANTLY SPICED CHICKPEA STEW

INGREDIENTS

4 servings

1 red onion
1 white onion
4 garlic cloves
2 tsp ras el hanout seasoning
1 tin of chopped tomatoes
1 tsp cinnamon
8 fresh mint leaves
2 tbsp pine nuts
a small handful of fresh coriander
chickpeas, cooked (230g)
dried apricots (50g)
coconut oil

METHOD

1. Heat a little coconut oil in a saucepan. Add chopped onions (both red and white) and garlic. Sauté for a few minutes before adding the chickpeas, ras el hanout and cinnamon.

2. After 5 minutes, stir in the chopped tomatoes and mix well. Place the lid on the pan and leave to cook on a low heat for 20-25 minutes.

3. Add chopped mint, coriander and apricots to the pan, mix everything together then finish on a low heat for 5 minutes.

4. Sprinkle with toasted pine nuts before serving. I like to eat mine served with tabbouleh, cucumber, fried plantain and lettuce mixed into coconut yoghurt.

CHILLI BEANS

INGREDIENTS

6-8 servings

1 red onion
1 white onion
6 garlic cloves
1 red pepper
1 courgette
1 tbsp cumin seeds
1 tsp ground ginger
1 tbsp smoked paprika
1 celery stick
3 tbsp tamari sauce
1 tbsp tomato paste
½ litre of vegetable stock
1 scotch bonnet pepper
2 potatoes
jalapeños (50g)
shiitake mushrooms (150g)
button mushrooms (150g)
pistachio nuts (100g)
kidney beans, tinned (240g)
black beans, tinned (240g)
cannellini beans, tinned (240g)
coconut oil

METHOD

1 Heat the coconut oil in a large saucepan then add chopped onions and the cumin seeds. Sauté for 2-3 minutes before adding chopped red pepper, courgette, jalapeno, celery and mushrooms. Next, place the smoked paprika, ginger, sea salt, black pepper and tamari sauce into the pan and mix well.

2 Stir the mixture for 5 minutes and then add the vegetable stock, tomato paste, kidney beans, black beans, cannellini beans, scotch bonnet pepper and diced potatoes.

Bring to the boil and leave on a medium heat for 45 minutes, stirring occasionally.

3 Meanwhile, spread the pistachio kernels onto a baking tray and roast in the oven on a high heat for 7- 8 minutes. Once roasted, add the pistachios to the chilli beans at any time.

HARD FOOD CURRY

This dish reminds me of my Grandad and my Auntie Doris, may they both rest in peace.

INGREDIENTS

6-8 servings

3 onions
1 Scotch bonnet pepper
1 springs onion
1 carrot
2 tomatoes
1 tbsp pimento seeds
1 tbsp ground ginger
8 sprigs of fresh thyme
4 tbsp curry powder
1 red pepper
1 cho cho (also known as chayote)
2 green bananas
1 sweet potato
10 garlic cloves, crushed
yellow yam (250g)
pumpkin (250g)
coconut oil
peppercorns
sea salt

METHOD

1 Heat 1 tbsp of coconut oil in a large saucepan. Add chopped onions, garlic, carrot and red pepper to the pan and season with crushed peppercorns and sea salt.

Sauté for 2-3 minutes before adding chopped tomatoes followed by the pimento seeds, ginger, curry powder, thyme and about a litre of water.

2 Stir the mixture together on a medium heat and bring to the boil. In the meantime, wash, peel and cut the yam, pumpkin, cho cho, bananas and sweet potato into cubes and add to the boiling mixture along with whole scotch bonnet pierced with a knife. Mix well then leave on a medium heat, stirring often.

3 After 30-40 minutes the mixture should begin to thicken and the yam, sweet potato, cho cho and bananas should be soft. Turn off the heat and allow to cool before serving. For the fullest flavour, leave the curry overnight and eat the next day.

FRIED DUMPLINGS

INGREDIENTS

Makes 6-8

¾ tsp salt
1 tsp cinnamon
1 tbsp butter, softened
grapeseed oil
self raising flour (200g)
coconut milk (50ml)
water (100ml)

METHOD

1 Add the flour to a large bowl with salt, cinnamon and softened butter. Combine with fingers until the butter is fully incorporated into the flour.

2 Pour in coconut milk and water and stir together until a dough is formed. Knead the dough with your hands for 2-3 minutes then leave to one side.

3 Break off small pieces of dough and roll together in your hands to shape into balls, lightly patting either end to finish. Remember the dough will expand during cooking so don't make the balls too big.

4 Heat a frying pan with a generous amount of oil on a medium heat to shallow fry the dumplings. When the oil is hot, place the dumplings in the pan and cook evenly on each side until golden.

PLANTAIN, CARROT & TOMATO SOUP

INGREDIENTS

2-3 servings

5 tomatoes
2 ripe plantains
6 garlic cloves
1 jalapeño pepper
carrots (200g)
coconut milk (200ml)
olive oil
sea salt
black pepper

METHOD

1 Place peeled and chopped plantains and carrots into a baking tray with tomatoes, garlic and chopped jalapeño pepper. Everything will be blended together so you don't need to be neat.

Drizzle the vegetables with olive oil, salt and pepper then roast in the oven on 220°c for 20 minutes.

2 Once cooked, tip the entire contents of the baking tray into a high-speed blender. Top with the coconut milk and water, to just above the level of the roasted vegetable contents.

3 Blend until smooth then serve.

Plantain, carrot & tomato soup topped with sun-dried tomatoes, cress and black pepper.

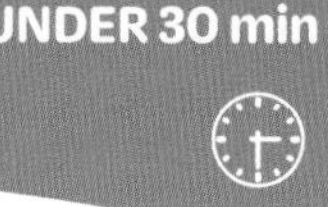

PILAU CHICKPEAS

This isn't really a recipe, instead it's a way to put together a tasty meal with minimal effort in just 15 minutes.

WHAT I USED

2 tbsp pilau seasoning
tenderstem broccoli
avocado
hummus
cucumber
lettuce
gluten-free pitta bread
chickpeas, tinned (240g)
olives
tomatoes
seasoning
sea salt
black pepper

METHOD

1 Drain, rinse and dry the chickpeas then place in a baking tray. Sprinkle the chickpeas with olive oil followed by the pilau rice seasoning, salt and pepper. Massage the seasoning into the chick-peas and cook in a preheated oven on 200°c for 10 minutes.

2 Wash and dry the broccoli then spread across a baking tray. Scatter over olive oil, salt and pepper then massage into the broccoli. Cook in the oven for 6-7 minutes.

3 Whilst both dishes cook in the oven, prepare a plate with the lettuce, cucumber, avocado, hummus, olives and tomatoes. Finish with toasted pitta bread and the cooked chickpeas and broccoli from the oven.

BUTTER BEAN STEW with mushrooms & Scotch bonnet pepper

INGREDIENTS

3-4 servings

1 onion
5 garlic cloves
2 carrots
1 red pepper
2 Scotch bonnet peppers
2 to 3 sprigs of fresh thyme
1 tin chopped tomatoes
mushrooms (240g)
vegetable stock (200ml)
coconut milk (200ml)
butter beans, cooked (240g)
fresh callaloo or spinach (100g)
coconut oil
black pepper
sea salt

Optional

1½ tsp jerk paste
red wine (100ml)

Butter bean stew, mixed pepper quinoa, cavolo nero, plantain fritters and hummus.

METHOD

1 Heat some oil in a large saucepan over a medium heat. Add chopped onions and garlic plus salt and pepper then sauté for 2-3 minutes.

2 Next place chopped carrots and red pepper into the pan with a deseeded finely chopped Scotch bonnet pepper and fresh thyme. Mix together for 2-3 minutes before stirring in chopped mushrooms, the optional red wine plus a little water to stop the mixture sticking to the pan.

3 Once the mushrooms are soft, pour in the vegetable stock, chopped tomatoes, coconut milk, butter beans and optional jerk paste then leave to simmer.

4 Pierce the other Scotch bonnet pepper with a sharp knife and add it to the stew with half a cup of water. Reduce the heat to low, place the lid on the pan and leave to cook for 45 minutes. Keep stirring the stew gently throughout so the Scotch bonnet pepper doesn't burst.

5 Once 45 minutes have passed, rinse and stir in the callaloo then turn off the heat, place the lid on the pan and leave the callaloo to wilt. Remove the scotch bonnet pepper before serving.

PLANTAIN FRITTERS

Make these with extra ripe plantains you might otherwise consider throwing away. When plantains turn ripe they go black – the black ones are the ones you want for this.

INGREDIENTS

4 servings

1 ripe plantain
½ onion
½ Scotch bonnet pepper
coconut oil
white spelt flour (or plain) (60g)
oat milk (50ml)
grated nutmeg
sea salt

METHOD

1 Peel then mash the plantain with the back of a fork or a potato masher. Place the mashed plantain in a bowl, add flour and oat milk then whisk together.

2 Next add finely chopped onions, thinly sliced and deseeded Scotch bonnet pepper, a few grates of nutmeg and a pinch of sea salt. Mix well.

3 Place a frying pan on a medium heat and pour in enough oil to generously cover the surface of the pan. Once hot, spoon in the mixture allowing 1 tablespoon of mixture per fritter.

Use the back of the spoon to roughly press the mixture into a circular fritter shape. Fry for 2-3 minutes on each side until golden. Press down each fritter with a spatula during cooking to ensure they are cooked all the way through.

ROASTED BUTTERNUT SQUASH

INGREDIENTS

4 servings

1	butternut squash
1	to 2 tbsp of sesame seeds
	sea salt
	black pepper
	toasted sesame oil

METHOD

1 Peel, deseed and dice the butternut squash- into cubes. Place in a large bowl with the salt, black pepper, sesame seeds and a drizzle of toasted sesame oil.

2 Mix everything together so the squash is evenly covered then spread the squash onto a baking tray.

3 Cook the squash in a preheated oven at 200°c for 15 minutes, until the squash is soft and fork tender.

LENTILS & CALLALOO

INGREDIENTS

4 servings

1 onion
5 garlic cloves
1 tsp dried thyme
1 tsp allspice
1 to 2 tsp cayenne pepper
3 to 4 bay leaves
2 tomatoes
coconut oil
callaloo, tinned (280g)
green lentils, cooked (230g)
sea salt

Optional

1 Scotch bonnet pepper

METHOD

1 If you're using tinned callaloo, drain, rinse and squeeze out as much water as possible. Place in a lightly greased frying pan and cook on a medium to high heat for 5 minutes, stirring constantly to remove as much water as possible.

2 Heat another saucepan with a little oil, add chopped onion and garlic, shortly followed by the dried thyme, allspice, cayenne pepper, bay leaves and sea salt. After a few minutes, add diced tomatoes and mix everything together for 5 minutes until the tomatoes begin to break up.

3 Stir in drained and rinsed green lentils, followed by the callaloo from the other pan and mix everything together. Finally add an optional, pierced Scotch bonnet pepper and cook on a low heat for 10 minutes with the lid on, adding a little water if necessary.

4 Remove the Scotch bonnet pepper before serving

Lentils and callaloo with island omelette fritters, steamed broccoli, roasted butternut squash and avocado.

RED LENTIL DAHL
with chickpeas & green banana

INGREDIENTS

4 servings

1 tsp turmeric
1 tbsp cumin seeds
8 whole cloves
1 large onion
5 garlic cloves
1 tsp chilli powder
1 tbsp curry powder
1 tsp ground coriander
1 cinnamon stick
4 bay leaves
1 tin chopped tomatoes
1 tbsp dairy-free butter
2 green bananas
red lentils (250g)
grapeseed oil
sea salt
chickpeas (250g), cooked
coconut milk (150ml)
small handful of fresh coriander
cracked black pepper

Red lentil dahl, rice and peas remixed, callaloo and onions, roasted cho cho, fried dumplings and fried plantain.

METHOD

1 Rinse and drain the lentils in a saucepan 5-6 times until the water is clear. Fill the pan with freshwater, stopping 2cm above the lentils. Stir in 1 tsp of salt plus ½ tsp turmeric and leave to cook on a medium heat for 20-25 minutes, stirring occasionally until soft. If the lentils begin to dry out, add a little water to the pan.

2 In a large saucepan, ideally one that's large enough to eventually hold the lentils, heat a drizzle of oil. Add the cumin seeds and whole cloves followed by finely chopped onions and chopped/crushed garlic. Sauté for a 2-3 minutes then stir in the chilli powder, curry powder, ground coriander, cinnamon stick, bay leaves and ½ tsp turmeric.

Mix everything together then stir in the chopped tomatoes and butter. Give it a final mix and leave to simmer for 5-6 minutes.

3 Drain the cooked lentils in a large sieve to remove any excess water then add them to the tomato mixture and mix well.

4 Peel and chop the green bananas and add them to the pan followed by the chickpeas and coconut milk. Season with a pinch of salt and pepper then leave to simmer on a low-medium heat for 15- 20 minutes until the banana has softened, stirring frequently. Once cooked, mix in the chopped coriander and allow to cool slightly before serving.

ACKEE & POTATO CURRY

INGREDIENTS

4 servings

1 onion
5 garlic cloves
1 tbsp cumin seeds
2 spring onions
2 large tomatoes
1 red pepper
2 tbsp curry powder
1 tbsp cinnamon
1 finely chopped deseeded Scotch bonnet pepper (optional)
potatoes, peeled (500g)
coconut milk (400ml)
small handful of fresh coriander
ackee, drained (540g)
sea salt
black pepper
coconut oil

METHOD

1 Heat a saucepan with coconut oil and add cumin seeds followed by finely chopped onion, minced/chopped garlic, a pinch of salt and black pepper. Sauté on a low heat until the onions soften.

2 Stir in the chopped tomatoes, spring onions, red pepper, scotch bonnet, cinnamon and curry powder. Allow to cook for a few minutes before adding the coconut milk and cubed potatoes. Leave on a rolling simmer with lid on, stirring occasionally until the potatoes have softened for 20-25 minutes.

3 Finally gently fold in the ackee and leave on a low heat for a further 5 minutes before topping with coriander. Allow to cool before serving.

Ackee and potato curry with cornmeal dumplings, boiled cho cho, avocado and fried plantain.

CORNMEAL DUMPLINGS

INGREDIENTS

makes 8 dumplings

1 tsp coconut sugar
1 tsp sea salt
1 tsp baking powder
½ tsp turmeric
1 tsp mild chilli powder
2 tbsp olive oil
fine cornmeal (100g)
coconut yoghurt (170g)
white spelt or plain flour (100g)
lukewarm water

METHOD

1 Mix all the dry ingredients together in a large bowl (ie. Everything except the yoghurt, oil and water).

2 Whisk the yoghurt into the dry ingredients until a dough begins to form, using a small amount of water to incorporate the last bits of flour.

Knead the dough for 2-3 minutes then shape into a soft ball. Rub the surface of the ball of dough with a little oil, cover and leave in the fridge for 15-20 minutes so the dough is easier to handle later.

3 Cover the surface of a shallow frying pan with oil and place on a medium heat. Take the dough out of the fridge, tear off a small piece (roughly 50g) and roll into a ball in the palm of your hand.

4 Press the ball between your palms to flatten it into a dumpling shape then place it into the hot pan. Repeat this step until all the dumplings are formed, ensuring the pan is not too crowded. There should be ample space around each dumpling for it to cook properly. Cook the dumplings on each side and around the edges for a few minutes, until golden.

ACKEE, LENTIL & BEAN CURRY

INGREDIENTS

4 servings

1 tsp cumin seeds
1 onion
5 garlic cloves
1 to 2 tsp thyme
2 tomatoes
1 tsp ginger, ground or freshly grated
½ tsp turmeric
1 tsp cayenne pepper
3 small sticks of lemongrass
½ lime
coconut milk (200ml)
kidney beans, tinned (100g)
green lentils, tinned (100g)
ackee, tinned (200g)
small handul of fresh coriander
grapeseed oil
sea salt

METHOD

1 Heat a little oil in a frying pan over a medium heat. Add the cumin seeds followed by chopped onions and garlic. Sauté for 2-3 minutes.

2 Next stir in chopped tomatoes followed by the ginger, turmeric, sea salt, cayenne pepper and lemongrass. (Crush the lemongrass stick between your chopping board and knife first to help the flavours escape during cooking).

3 Add the coconut milk, kidney beans and lentils then mix well. Leave on a medium to low heat with the lid on, stirring occasionally.

4 After 10 minutes, gently mix in the drained and rinsed ackee followed by the chopped coriander. Cook for a few minutes then leave to cool. Serve with a squeeze of lime juice.

5 Remove the Scotch bonnet pepper before serving.

Ackee and kidney bean curry with spiced potato cakes, fried plantain, avocado and roti.

SPICED POTATO CAKES

INGREDIENTS

Makes 8-10 potato cakes

4 medium sized potatoes, skin on
1 onion
4 garlic cloves
1 tbsp ground coriander
1 tsp ground turmeric
1 tsp chilli powder
1 tsp dairy-free butter (optional)
1 tomato
1 tbsp cinnamon cracked
2 to 3 tbsp fresh coriander
4 tbsp spelt or plain flour
½ lemon, juiced
1½ tsp fresh ginger
1½ tbsp mustard seeds
1½ tbsp cumin seeds
grapeseed oil
black pepper
sea salt

METHOD

1 Rinse the potatoes and cut into cubes. Place in a pan of fresh water with a tablespoon of sea salt then leave to boil for 10-15 minutes until the potatoes are fork tender but not too soft. Gently tip the potatoes into a colander to drain off the water then leave to one side to cool and dry out.

2 Heat a drizzle of oil in a saucepan on a medium heat. Toast the mustard seeds and cumin seeds for a minute before adding finely chopped onion and garlic. Next stir in the fresh ginger, ground coriander, turmeric, chilli powder and dairy-free butter. Mix together for 2-3 minutes then pour in finely diced tomato and the cinnamon. Leave on a low heat until a paste-like texture is formed.

3 Place the potatoes in a large bowl and mash well. Having cooled, the potatoes should have some firmness to them so mashing may take a little work. Add the tomato mixture to the mashed potatoes followed by the lemon juice and fresh coriander. Season with black pepper and sea salt then mix well.

Sprinkle over 2 tablespoons of flour and mix everything together until fully combined. Cover the mixture with a tea towel and leave in the freezer for 25 minutes or the fridge for 45 minutes. Cooling the mixture will help the potato cakes to hold their shape.

4 Roughly cover a large plate with 2 tbsp of flour to a large plate, roughly covering the surface. Take a meatball-sized piece of potato mix, roll into a ball then around in the flour so that it is fully covered. Flatten the ball between your hands and shape it into a patty shape with your finger and thumb.

5 Heat a generous amount of oil in a frying pan. Once hot, shallow fry the potato cakes 2-3 at a time, cooking for 2-3 minutes on each side until golden. Place the cooked cakes onto a paper towel to remove any excess oil before serving. Alternatively, cook the potato cakes in the oven for 30 minutes at 180°c.

FOR THE LOVE OF PLANTAIN

Plantain (pronounced "plan-tin" in Jamaica) is my all-time favourite ingredient.

Every cuisine has a hero food, when it comes to Caribbean cooking, plantain is mine.

Plantain is a delicious, versatile and nutritious ingredient which makes everything taste better. A staple throughout the Caribbean, Africa, South America and much of Asia, it may look a little similar to the small, yellow Cavendish bananas we eat daily but that's where the similarity ends.

With its complex flavour that's a moreish combination of savoury and sweet, plantain can act as a range of carbohydrates or even flour, in your cooking. Adaptable and succulent, it's an essential ingredient in Caribbean cooking you'll grow to love.

Containing less sugar and starch than a potato, plantain is packed with antioxidants and potassium. A firm yet juicy texture means it's ideal for frying, boiling, roasting and working into an infinite number of dishes. Its versatility, gorgeous flavour and low cost means plantain is increasingly used in Western cooking and plantain crisps can be found on sale in most shops in the UK.

The consistency and taste of a plantain changes as it ripens so it is more suited to certain dishes than others at different stages of ripening.

As it grows, a plantain is green and firm. When picked from the tree at this stage, the maturing process is halted and these plantains are likely to remain green. Green plantain is much harder in texture and packed with iron. It can be used to make crisps, porridge, flour and tostones.

As plantain ripens, its colour deepens from a sunny dark yellow to a deep browny- black in patches that spread across the skin. When fully ripe, a plantain looks almost black and is soft and sweet inside. These blackened, sweet plantains are perfect for making pancakes and fritters.

Before a plantain is completely ripe, the skin will begin to darken although yellow patches will still be visible. I use plantain at this stage of ripening for most of my cooking because the consistency is ideal for frying and baking.

Plantains ripen quickly so it's best to buy them when they are yellow in colour with only a few black marks on the skin. Depending on the environment they are in, plantains usually take around seven days to ripen.

PLANTAIN PANCAKES with orange, cinnamon & allspice

INGREDIENTS

Makes 6-8 pancakes

1 ripe plantain
1 tbsp cinnamon
1 tsp baking powder
½ tsp allspice
1 tbsp coconut sugar
1 tbsp orange extract
2 tbsp olive oil
oat milk (150ml)
white spelt flour (90g)

METHOD

1 Mash the plantain as smooth as possible - I find it's easiest if you use the back of a fork on a plate or flat surface.

Place the mashed plantain in a large mixing bowl. Add the cinnamon, baking powder, allspice and coconut sugar then mix all the ingredients together.

2 Whisk in the oat milk followed by the spelt flour to form a soft mixture then beat in the orange extract and olive oil. The mixture should pour with ease but still have a slight thickness to it. The flour to milk ratio may vary depending on the size of the plantain you use so if the mixture is too thick, add a little more milk - if it's too runny, add a little more flour.

3 Place a non-stick frying pan on a medium heat without any oil. Pour the mixture into the pan to form rough circles, starting from the centre of each pancake. Once air bubbles begin to appear on the surface of the pancake, flip it over and cook for a further 1-2 minutes.

4 Serve the pancakes stacked with your favourite pancake toppings or sides. Alternatively, eat the pancakes as a savoury side dish as part of a main meal.

Smoky ackee and chickpeas with: butter bean stew, shiitake mushrooms, tomatoes, grilled courgette, roasted cashew nuts, avocado, smoked h ummus and plantain pancakes.

JOLLOF-INSPIRED RICE

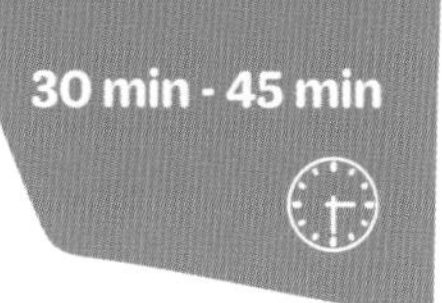

INGREDIENTS

6 servings

2 red peppers
2 tomatoes
1 red onion
1 white onion
4 garlic cloves
1 tbsp coconut oil
1 tbsp jollof seasoning
1 Scotch bonnet pepper
olive oil
water (200ml)
basmati rice (500g)
sea salt

Scrambled smoked tofu and chickpeas with: jollof-inspired rice, roasted broccoli, roasted cho cho, fried plantain, sautéed baby mushrooms and hummus.

METHOD

1 Place roughly chopped red peppers, tomatoes, onions and garlic on a baking tray. Drizzle with a little olive oil and cook in a preheated oven at 200°c (fan) for 20 minutes or until light charring is visible.

Leave to cool then blend in a high speed blender with the water and Scotch bonnet pepper, until smooth.

2 In a large saucepan, wash and drain the rice 2-3 times until the water is clear. Fill the pan with fresh water, stopping 1cm above the rice. Place the pan on a medium heat and stir in the coconut oil, jollof seasoning and 1-2 tsp of sea salt.

3 Once the rice begins to boil, reduce the heat and gently stir the mixture from the blender into the rice. Replace the lid and leave to cook on a low heat.

4 After 10 minutes, gently stir the rice to stop it sticking to the bottom of the pan. If the bottom of the pan seems dry, create a small well in the centre of the rice with a fork and pour 40-50ml of water into the hole so it flows directly to the bottom of the pan. Place the lid back on the pan and cook for a further 5 minutes on a low heat. After 5 minutes, turn off the heat and leave the rice to continue to steam in the pan for another 10 minutes.

SCRAMBLED TOFU
with chickpeas

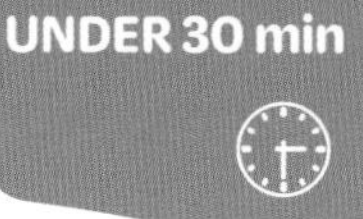

INGREDIENTS

2 servings

1	tsp berbere spice
½	turmeric
1	tsp cayenne pepper
½	tsp sea salt
1	tsp tomato paste
1	tomato
	chickpeas, tinned (120g)
	coconut oil
	smoked tofu (140g), the firm type

METHOD

1 Dry any excess water from the tofu then crumble into a mixing bowl. Add the berbere spice, turmeric, cayenne pepper, sea salt, tomato paste and a drizzle of oil. Combine gently so the tofu is evenly covered.

2 Heat a frying pan with a little oil, add the tofu mix and sauté for 6-7 minutes.

3 Stir in the chopped tomatoes and chickpeas then mix well. Add a little water if necessary, to stop the mixture sticking to the pan. Cook on a low - medium heat for a further 5 minutes, stirring occasionally.

ROASTED CHO CHO
(or chayote / christophenes)

INGREDIENTS

1 cho cho
olive oil
sea salt
cracked black pepper

METHOD

1 Rinse the cho cho then cut in half lengthways (you can choose to cook it with or without the skin on). Remove the seed from both halves with a knife then cut the cho cho into slices.

2 Place the slices into a bowl, drizzle with a little olive oil and season with a pinch of salt and a sprinkle of cracked black pepper.

3 Line a baking tray with parchment paper and spread the cho cho evenly across the tray. Roast in a preheated oven at 200°c for 10 minutes or until soft.

Roasting cho cho with a little olive oil, sea salt and cracked black pepper is delicious. For a twist, try adding a little cinnamon too.

BUSS UP SHUT ROTI

I have adapted this recipe so it can be cooked in a standard frying pan as I imagine many of you, like myself, do not have a traditional Tawa in your kitchen cupboard.

INGREDIENTS

8 rotis

½ tsp sea salt
1 tbsp coconut sugar
2 tsp baking powder
1 tsp olive oil
spelt flour (300g)
lukewarm water
dairy-free butter/coconut oil, melted (30-40g)

METHOD

1 Mix together all the dry ingredients in a large bowl.

2 Add small amounts of lukewarm water and mix to begin to form a dough. Before the mixture is fully combined, add cooled, melted butter or coconut oil, then knead the mixture until it forms a soft, firm dough. If the dough is too sticky add a little flour and knead until smooth.

3 Drop a teaspoon of olive oil over the surface of the dough and knead lightly until the oil is absorbed. Cover the ball of dough with a tea towel and leave in the fridge to rest for 20 minutes so the dough is easy to shape.

4 Place the dough onto a well-floured surface and cut into 8 equal pieces (this will produce rotis that fit perfectly into a standard sized frying pan).

5 To form each loyah:

Take one piece of dough in the palm of your hand and press into a circular shape. Put the dough back onto the floured surface, dust with a little flour and roll into a thin circle, flipping the dough over as you roll for an even finish.

Don't roll the dough so thin that it breaks when handled or worry about making it into a perfect circle. The finished dough should be a couple of millimetres thick like a thin pastry case. Brush the top of the dough with coconut oil, butter or a mixture of both.

6 To make the cone-shape:

Place the tip of a blunt knife into the centre of the circle and cut a straight line from the centre to the edge of the dough to form an opening.

Lift the tip of one of the openings and fold over to create a triangle, leaving roughly three quarters of the dough remaining. Continue folding the dough over in (roughly) equal-sized triangles, working in an anti-clockwise direction until you reach the other end.

Finish your loyah by tucking in the sticking out corners at the bottom of your cone-shaped dough and gently pushing the top down into the centre. Leave your finished loyah to rest underneath a tea towel so it doesn't dry out whilst you shape the rest of your loyahs.

7 To cook your loyahs:

Flatten one of the loyahs on a floured surface with the palm of your hand, using your fingers to push the edges out into a circular shape. Dust lightly with flour and roll evenly into a circle, sprinkling with flour as needed to prevent the dough from sticking.

Lightly brush a non-stick frying pan with oil or butter and heat on a medium hob until hot. Carefully place the flattened loyah into the hot pan (don't worry if any edges end up slightly folded over) and flip every 30 seconds until golden brown spots appear.

Brush the top of the roti with oil or butter each time you flip it over. When the roti is almost ready, use a spatula and wooden spoon to push the edges of the roti into the middle of the pan then slap it between the utensils a few times to "buss it up" and create its signature soft, flaky layers.

JOLLOF RICE & PEAS FUSION

Two of the best rice dishes on the globe, fused together in one dish. No words.

INGREDIENTS

6 servings

1 red pepper
1 tin chopped tomatoes
1 Scotch bonnet pepper
5 garlic cloves
1 onion
1 tbsp dairy-free butter
2 to 3 sprigs of fresh thyme
1 to 2 tsp sea salt
basmati rice (500g)
creamed coconut (50g)
kidney beans, tinned (230g)

Red pea stew with: jollof rice and peas fusion, roasted squash, fried plantain, buss up shot roti, roasted cho cho and quinoa.

METHOD

1 Place the red pepper, tomatoes, Scotch bonnet pepper, garlic and onion into a high speed blender and blend until smooth.

2 Wash and drain the rice 2-3 times in a large saucepan until the water is clear. Fill the pan with fresh water, stopping 1cm above the rice then place on a medium heat. Drain and rinse the kidney beans then add to the pan followed by the butter, salt, creamed coconut and thyme then give everything a good mix.

3 Once the rice begins to boil, reduce the heat to low and gently fold the mixture from the blender into the rice. Top the pan with a lid and leave on a low heat.

4 After 10 minutes, gently stir the rice to stop it sticking to the bottom of the pan. If the bottom of the pan seems dry, create a small well in the centre of the rice with a fork and pour 40-50ml of water into the hole so it goes directly to the bottom of the pan.

5 Place the lid back on and cook for a further 5 minutes on a low heat. After 5-8 minutes the heat can be turned off. Leave the rice with the lid on for a further 10 minutes to allow the rice to continue to cook in its steam.

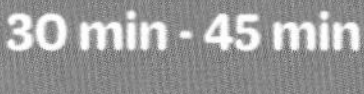

ISLAND OMELETTE

INGREDIENTS

2-3 omelettes

2 tsp baking powder
1 tsp sea salt
2 tsp dried thyme
1 to 2 tsp ground ginger
½ tsp ground cloves
4 garlic cloves
4 spring onions
1 Scotch bonnet pepper, deseeded
water (approx 250ml)
steamed pumpkin (100g)
chickpea flour (gram flour) (170g)
coconut oil

METHOD

1 Peel and chop the pumpkin into small cubes and steam until soft.

2 In a large mixing bowl, add the chickpea flour, baking powder, sea salt, thyme, ground ginger and ground cloves then mix together.

Next add water and mix together to form a batter. Stir in the crushed/chopped garlic, finely chopped spring onions and thinly sliced Scotch bonnet pepper (without the seeds unless you want it to be spicy).

3 Mash the steamed pumpkin with the back of a fork and add to the mixture.

4 Cover the surface of a frying pan with oil then place on the heat. Put 1 tablespoon of mixture into the pan and fry for 2 minutes on each side until golden.

Island omelette served with peri peri sweet potato fries, hummus, avocado, tomato salsa, steamed spring greens and plantain.

TOSTONES (fried green plantain)

This is one of the tastiest ways to use green plantain. Green plantain tastes completely different to the sweet yellow plantains that we're more familiar with.

INGREDIENTS

Approx. 8 pieces

green plantain
coconut oil
sea salt
cracked black pepper
nutmeg

METHOD

1 Peel and slice the plantain 1cm thick and shallow fry until slightly golden on each side. Remove the plantain from the pan, place on a paper towel and allow to cool.

2 Now flatten your plantain coins. You can do this by placing the plantain onto a chopping board and pressing down hard with something that has a flat surface, like the back of a plate or a glass.

Sprinkle the plantain with a little sea salt and pepper. I also like to add a dash of nutmeg for an extra touch of flavour.

3 Add a little oil to a pan and place on the heat. Put the flattened coins of plantain into the pan and fry until golden on both sides. When they are ready, remove the plantain from the pan and place on a paper towel.

Tostones with ackee and chickpeas, callaloo, fried breadfruit and avocado.

JACKFRUIT, BLACK BEAN & SWEET POTATO CURRY

1 HOUR

INGREDIENTS

4 servings

1 large sweet potato
2 onions
8 cardamon pods
1 tsp mustard seeds
1 tsp cumin seeds
5 garlic cloves
1 tbsp ginger, chopped/grated
2 tbsp curry powder
1 tomato
1 tsp cayenne pepper
1 tsp coconut sugar
½ lime
2 to 3tbsp fresh coriander
black beans, tinned (230g)
coconut milk (400g)
young jackfruit (400g)

Jackfruit, black bean and sweet potato curry, plantain fritters, boiled cho cho, green banana and pumpkin.

METHOD

1 Drain and rinse the jackfruit. Dry off any excess water and shred the jackfruit with your fingers. Place in a bowl and leave to one side.

2 Peel and cube a large sweet potato and steam until fork tender. Don't let it go too soft because it will finish cooking in the curry.

3 Heat a frying pan with a little oil, add chopped onions and mix for 8-10 minutes until the onions begin to brown. Stir in the crushed cardamon pods, mustard seeds and cumin seeds then sauté for 3-4 minutes until the seeds begin to crackle.

Chop the garlic and add to the pan with the ginger, curry powder, chopped tomato, sea salt and cayenne pepper then mix for 2- 3 minutes so everything is combined. Add a little water if necessary to avoid the mixture sticking to the pan.

4 Pour in the coconut milk, coconut sugar and lime juice followed by drained and rinsed black beans, steamed sweet potato and shredded jackfruit. Gently combine everything together then add a little water. Place on a low heat, sprinkle with coriander and leave to simmer for 15 minutes, stirring occasionally.

30 min - 45 min

SMOKY ACKEE & CHICKPEAS

INGREDIENTS

4 servings

2 tsp smoked paprika
1 tsp dried thyme
1 tsp cracked
1 red pepper
1 large onion
4 garlic cloves
2 spring onions
1 tsp dried thyme
1 small leek
1 red pepper
⅓ tsp jerk paste
1 tbsp coconut cream
2 tbsp tomato ketchup
1 tomato
½ tsp allspice
1 tbsp smoked hummus
chickpeas, tinned (230g)
ackee, tinned (540g)
black pepper
olive oil
sea salt

Smoky ackee and chickpeas with rice and peas, roasted broccoli, fried plantain and avocado.

METHOD

1 Rinse and drain the chickpeas then place in a mixing bowl. Add the smoked paprika, a pinch of salt, dried thyme, black pepper and a drizzle of oil then mix together. Spread the chickpeas evenly across a baking tray lined with greaseproof paper, add diced red pepper and place in the oven at 180°c for 15 minutes.

2 Heat a little oil in a frying pan on a medium heat. Add chopped onions, garlic, spring onions and leek followed by the dried thyme, sea salt, black pepper and jerk paste. Leave to sauté for 4-5 minutes, adding a little water if necessary to avoid the mixture sticking to the pan.

3 Stir the roasted chickpea and red pepper mixture into the pan and stir everything together. Pour in the coconut cream, tomato ketchup, chopped tomato, smoked hummus and allspice. Mix together for a 2-3 minutes then add drained and rinsed ackee. Gently combine the ackee with the rest of the ingredients to avoid crushing the ackee.

4 Continue to cook on a low heat for 4-5 minutes then turn off the heat, top with a lid and leave for a further 5 minutes before serving.

SOUTHERN FRIED CAULIFLOWER

INGREDIENTS

1 head of cauliflower
1 tsp smoked paprika
1 tbsp black pepper
1 tsp cayenne pepper
1 tsp dried thyme
1 tbsp herbes de Provence
1 tbsp baking powder
1 tsp onion powder
1 tsp nutmeg
4 to 5 tbsp chickpeas
self-raising flour (120g)
flour (gram flour)
oat milk (150ml)
grapeseed oil

METHOD

1 Slice "steaks" from the cauliflower head, starting from the stalk of the cauliflower. You can usually get at least 2 pieces from one head. Gently wash and dry each steak thoroughly then leave to one side.

2 In a shallow bowl, whisk together the chick-pea flour and oat milk (don't worry if it ends up a little lumpy).

3 In another shallow bowl, mix together the self raising flour, paprika, garlic powder, black pepper, thyme, herbes de Provence, baking powder, onion powder and nutmeg.

4 Heat a frying pan with enough oil to shallow fry the cauliflower pieces. Gently place a cauliflower piece into the chickpea and milk mixture until it is evenly covered. Next, put the steak into the flour mixture and ensure the steak is fully coated.

5 Carefully place the steak into the hot frying pan and shallow fry on each side for 3 min-utes on a medium – high heat until golden.

6 You may choose to finish the steaks in the oven for maximum crisp. Put the cauliflower steaks onto a baking tray and cook in a pre-heated oven on 200°c (fan) for 10 minutes.

BLACK KALE FRITTERS

INGREDIENTS

Makes approx 10 fritters

3 black kale (also known as cavolo nero) leaves
3 to 4 tbsp of tamari
plain flour (200g)
self-raising flour (100g)
water (350ml)
black pepper
sea salt
grapeseed oil

METHOD

1 Heat a little grapeseed oil in a frying pan.

2 Chop the black kale into thin, shred-like strips and add to the frying pan. Sauté on a medium - high heat for 2 minutes then stir in the tamari and black pepper. Set aside and leave to cool.

3 In a bowl, mix together the flour, water. salt and pepper until a wet dough-like consistency is formed then stir in the cooled black kale.

4 Place a generous amount of grapeseed oil into a saucepan and heat on a medium setting. Ensure the base of the pan is fully covered.

5 With the pan still on a medium heat, spoon the fritter mixture into the pan leaving space between each fritter so they don't stick together. Fry each fritter for 2 minutes on each side or until golden.

COCONUT RICE

UNDER 30 min

INGREDIENTS

4-6 servings

2	cups basmati rice
1	tbsp coconut sugar
1	tbsp dairy-free butter
½	tsp salt
	coconut milk (200g)

METHOD

1 Rinse the rice in a saucepan of water then drain. Repeat roughly 5 times until the water begins to look clear.

2 Fill the pan with fresh water, stopping 1cm above the rice then cook on a high heat. Using a fork, gently stir in the coconut milk, coconut sugar, butter and salt, ensuring you don't over-stir the mixture.

3 Once it begins to boil, give the mixture a final stir, reduce the heat to low, top with a lid and leave to simmer for 15 minutes.

4 After 15 minutes, gently fluff the rice from the bottom up with a fork and turn off the heat. Replace the lid and leave to steam for the final 5 minutes of cooking time.

PLANTAIN & AVOCADO ON TOAST

INGREDIENTS

1	ripe avocado
½	lime, juiced pinch of salt
1	tsp black pepper
1	tsp chilli flakes
2	to 3 tbsp fresh coriander
1	plantain
2	slices of hard dough bread
1	tbsp coconut oil
	small handful of pumpkin seeds

METHOD

1. Add pumpkin seeds to a baking tray and place in the oven on a high heat for 4-5 minutes until the seeds begin to toast.

2. In a bowl, skin and mash the avocado with the lime juice, salt, black pepper, chilli flakes and coriander then mix well.

3. In a frying pan, heat a little coconut oil. Peel, cut and fry the plantain on each side until-golden.

4. Toast the bread or butter it and fry it on a griddle pan.

5. To serve, place the mashed avocado onto the toast, followed by the plantain slices and a sprinkle of toasted pumpkin seeds which you can use whole or crushed with a pestle and mortar.

GUINNESS PUNCH

INGREDIENTS

4 servings

1 tsp fresh nutmeg, grated
Guinness (440ml)
condensed coconut milk (160g)
cashew nuts (100g)
hemp milk (200ml)
splash of white rum

METHOD

1 Soak the cashew nuts overnight (or for at least an hour if you're short of time).

2 Pour the Guinness, 100ml hemp milk and condensed coconut milk into a large bowl and whisk together until the condensed milk is fully combined.

3 Blend the cashew nuts and the remaining 100ml of hemp milk in a high-speed blender until smooth and creamy.

4 Slowly stir the blended nut mix into the Guinness mixture and whisk until creamy.

5 To finish whisk in the grated nutmeg and a splash of white rum. The punch is best served chilled.

ACKEE

You'll find ackee used throughout this book. It's one of those versatile ingredients you can pop in the pan for a few minutes and always turn out a good meal. A subtle taste and smooth texture means you can pair ackee with just about any savoury ingredient.

First found in West Africa, ackee is a fruit known by many names across Africa and the world, including: ankye, achee, akee isin, and ackee apple. During the slave trade, ackee made its way to Jamaica and other islands across the Caribbean.

Ackee was passionately embraced in Jamaica where it enjoys an elevated status as the national fruit as well as one half of the country's national dish, ackee and saltfish. Ackee is grown all over Jamaica and can regularly be found growing in people's back gardens. Ackee and saltfish is a versatile dish, traditionally eaten as a special breakfast but often also eaten for dinner.

Ackee trees belong to the tropical Sapindaceae tree family, a species which includes lychees and rambutan. Similar to lychees and rambutan, ackee has a mellow flavour, striking red skin and soft, lightly coloured flesh.

Once ripe, the skin turns from green to a scarlet red with shades of bright orange and the three curved lobes open up to reveal three large, black round seeds, each with a creamy-looking, pale yellow, crescent-shaped segment attached, called an aril.

These segments are the only part of the ackee we eat, the rest is discarded. Ackee is a good source of carbohydrates, proteins and fats, making it perfect for cooking.

Ackee can only be eaten when ripe because the unripe fruit is highly poisonous with hypoglycin A and B.

Jamaica is the sole exporter of ackee so you can find tinned ackee on sale in most major UK supermarkets, Asian food shops and all Caribbean food stores.

CREAMY SQUASH & PLANTAIN SOUP

INGREDIENTS

6-8 servings

2 tbsp coconut oil
2 onions
4 garlic cloves
1 red pepper, chargrilled
2 tbsp tomato paste
2 ripe plantains
½ lemon, juiced
1 tsp sea salt
1 tsp black pepper
1 tsp chili flakes
Small handful of fresh coriander
Small handful of fresh parsley
fresh ginger (10g)
queen squash (400g)
mixed nuts (50g)
vegetable stock (200ml)
creamed coconut (50g)
coconut milk (300ml)

For the topping

1 plantain, peeled, fried and chopped
1 tbsp fresh coriander
1 tbsp spring onion
1 tbsp radish
sesame seeds
olive oil

METHOD

1 To chargrill the pepper: Place the red pepper in the oven for 20 minutes on a high heat and remove when the skin begins to darken in colour. Alternatively, put the pepper under the grill or on the barbecue, turning regularly for an even char.

2 Discard the skins of the garlic, ginger, onion and plantain. Roughly chop and dice all the vegetables, ensuring the squash is cut into small cubes so it cooks quickly.

3 Heat coconut oil in a large saucepan on a medium heat. Add chopped onions, garlic, ginger, squash cut into small cubes, tomato paste, plantain and mixed nuts stirring frequently to prevent the mixture sticking. Mix together for 4-5 minutes.

4 Next add the vegetable stock, creamed coconut, coconut milk, the charred red pepper, sea salt and black pepper. Mix together well and leave on a medium heat for 15 minutes . When the squash has softened, remove from the heat and blend on a high setting until smooth and creamy.

5 For the topping: Finely chop the coriander, spring onion and radish. Place the soup in bowls and top with ingredients finishing with a drizzle of olive oil to finish.

ORANGE PANCAKES

INGREDIENTS

Makes 6-8 pancakes

1½ cup spelt flour
2 tsp baking powder
1 tbsp cinnamon
1 tbsp coconut sugar
1 cup of coconut milk
2 tbsp orange extract
½ an orange, zested
coconut oil

METHOD

1 In a mixing bowl, add the flour, baking powder, cinnamon and coconut sugar. Mix together before pouring in the coconut milk, orange extract and orange zest. Stir the batter until smooth then leave to rest for 10 minutes before use.

2 Heat a tbsp of coconut oil in a frying pan on a low-medium heat.

3 Pour pancake-sized circles of the batter into the pan. When bubbles start to appear on the surface after 2 minutes, it's time to flip the pancakes over.

4 Serve the pancakes stacked, with your toppings of choice. I added desiccated coconut, maple syrup, lemon juice and more orange zest.

TRIPLE COOKED HERB POTATOES

45 min - 1 hour

INGREDIENTS

6 white potatoes (Maris Piper or Albert Rooster work best)
1 tbsp of dried rosemary
1 tbsp of dried thyme
1 tbsp of dairy-free butter
2 sprigs fresh thyme
1 tsp sea salt
1 tsp black pepper
extra virgin olive oil

METHOD

1 Roughly peel and cube the potatoes, leaving some skin on for texture and taste.

2 Rinse the potatoes in a saucepan of water. Refill the pan with fresh water, add the sea salt and fresh thyme then leave to boil.

3 As soon as the water begins to boil, remove the pan from the heat and pour the potatoes into a colander. The potatoes should hold their shape and feel firm.

4 Add the potatoes back to the empty saucepan with a generous drizzle of olive oil; adding the butter, dried rosemary, sea salt and black pepper. Mix together well, ensuring the potatoes are evenly coated.

5 Place the potatoes into a baking tray lined with parchment paper and spread evenly. Cook in a preheated oven on 200°c (fan) for 20-25 minutes until the potatoes are slightly golden and crispy on the outside. Don't forget to turn the potatoes halfway through the cooking time. The potatoes are delicious left just like this but the next step adds even more crispiness and colour.

6 Heat a frying pan with olive oil and add the cooked potatoes. Ensure the pan is not overfilled so the potatoes get a good crisp exterior. Sauté the potatoes until golden in colour.

ACKEE AND CHICKPEAS

INGREDIENTS

4 servings

1 tbsp coconut oil
5 garlic cloves
1 large onion
1 red pepper
2 spring onions
6 sprigs of fresh thyme
1 tsp dried thyme
1 tsp chilli flakes
1 tbsp black pepper
1 tsp sea salt
1 tsp Caribbean curry powder
½ Scotch bonnet pepper
1 tbsp dairy-free butter
2 tbsp coconut milk
1 tsp tomato puree
creamed coconut (50g)
cooked chickpeas, tinned (250g)
cherry tomatoes (120g)
ackee, tinned (340g)

METHOD

1 Heat the coconut oil in a frying pan on a medium heat. Add chopped garlic, onion, peppers and spring onions. Place the fresh thyme in the pan and mix the ingredients together for 2-3 minutes until the onions soften.

2 Next stir the chickpeas, chopped cherry tomatoes, dried thyme, chili flakes, black pepper, sea salt, curry powder and Scotch bonnet pepper de-seeded and finely chopped into the pan. Cook for 3-5 minutes, stirring often.

3 Add the butter, coconut milk, creamed coconut and tomato puree to the pan. Mix everything together then leave on a medium heat for 10-15 minutes, stirring often.

4 To finish, rinse the ackee in a colander, add it to the pan and stir it in gently so the ackee doesn't get crushed. After 2-3 minutes when the ackee is heated through, turn off the heat.

LIQUOR MUFFINS

My nan makes the best Christmas cake. She'd always leave a tub of raisins and currants soaking in alcohol for a whole year so she could make a cake packed with flavour.

To prepare the dried fruit: pour equal quantities of currants and raisins along with 2 parts of red wine and 1 part of white rum into a tightly sealed container. Ensure the raisins and currents are completely covered by the liquid and leave to soak in a cool, dry place.

INGREDIENTS

Makes 4-6 muffins

1 large ripe banana
2 tbsp cinnamon
1 tbsp orange extract
1 tbsp vanilla extract
4 tbsp raisins & currants soaked in rum and wine
1 tsp baking powder
4 to 6 muffin cases
dairy-free butter (100g)
brown sugar (70g)
self raising flour (120g)

METHOD

1. Place the butter and sugar in a mixing bowl and cream together with the back of a spoon.

2. In a separate bowl, use a fork to mash the peeled banana with the cinnamon until smooth.

3. Pour the mashed banana into the creamed butter and sugar. Mix well then sprinkle over the orange extract, vanilla extract, baking powder, currants and raisins.

4. Give the mixture a good stir before sieving in the self raising flour and mix again. You could also pour in a splash of rum here.

5. Spoon the mixture into the muffin cases leaving a 1cm space at the top of each case.

6. Place in a preheated oven on 180°c (fan) for 20 minutes. To check if the muffins are cooked, poke a knife through the centre. If there is muffin mixture left on the knife they may need a few more minutes.

SWEET POTATO FIRE PIE

A fiery sweet potato topping, seasoned with punchy cajun spices and smoked paprika, gives this dish character whilst the moreish lentil filling is packed with flavour, delivering a texture that's perfect.

INGREDIENTS

4-6 servings

1 white onion
1 red onion
3 carrots
5 garlic cloves
1 tsp sea salt
1 tbsp black pepper
1 tsp chilli flakes
1 tsp dried thyme
1 tsp dried rosemary
1 tbsp cornflour
2 to 3 tbsp vegan worcester sauce
1 tbsp tomato puree
Splash of red wine (optional)
vegetable stock (Vecon works best) (250ml)
chestnut mushrooms (250g)
green lentils, cooked (400g)
frozen garden peas (120g)
Small handful of fresh parsley
coconut oil

Sweet potato topping

1½ kg sweet potato
2 tsp smoked paprika
1 tbsp cajun spice mix
1 tsp sea salt

METHOD

1 Peel and chop the sweet potatoes then steam until soft. Drain off the excess water and leave to one side.

2 Heat coconut oil in a frying pan on a medium heat. Add chopped onions, garlic and carrots to the pan then stir for 2-3 minutes. Follow with the chopped mushrooms, green lentils and the frozen peas. Mix everything together for 2-3 minutes.

3 Season the mixture with the sea salt, black pepper, chilli flakes, chopped parsley, thyme and rosemary. Stir well then pour in the vegetable stock, worcester sauce, red wine and tomato puree. Mix well then place the cornflour in a cup filled with 75ml of water at room temperature.

Mix the cornflour and water together then stir it into the lentil mixture. Leave the mixture to cook on a low heat for 10 minutes, stirring occasionally. After 10 minutes, when the mixture has thickened, turn off the heat.

4 Mash your sweet potatoes until smooth. Add smoked paprika, cajan spice mix, sea salt and mix it into the potatoes.

5 Spread the pie mixture evenly across the bottom of an oven proof dish then top with the sweet potato mash. Use a fork to create ridges across the top. Place the pie under the grill for a few minutes until the peaks of the mashed potato topping are slightly crisp. Leave to cool before serving.

30 min - 45 min

NAN'S CORNMEAL PORRIDGE

There's nothing better than a hot, comforting bowl of my nan's cornmeal porridge with a soft slice of hard dough bread for dipping.

INGREDIENTS

4 servings

1 tsp vanilla extract
4 cinnamon leaves
fine cornmeal (200g)
1 litre water
pinch of salt
A few grates of fresh nutmeg

Sweetener options

condensed coconut milk
coconut sugar
maple syrup date syrup

METHOD

1 Pour the cornmeal and salt into a large saucepan then fill with 1 litre of water. Place the pan on a medium heat and stir continuously until the cornmeal begins to thicken.

Stirring is really important throughout because it prevents lumps forming.

2 Once the cornmeal has thickened, add the cinnamon leaves and top with a lid. Turn down the heat and leave to cook for 25 minutes, stirring occasionally.

3 After 25 minutes, turn off the heat and add vanilla extract plus the sweetener of your choice. For extra creaminess, add Barista oat milk until your preferred consistency is achieved.

SPICY FRIED RICE

This recipe will take your rice from bomb to bombacla**. These instructions begin from once the rice is cooked.

INGREDIENTS

- 4 garlic cloves
- 1 large onion
- ½ red pepper
- ½ green pepper
- ½ yellow pepper
- ½ Scotch bonnet pepper
- 1 tbsp dairy-free butter
- 1 tbsp of black pepper
- 3 to 4 tbsp of tamarind paste
- ¾ tsp jerk paste
- few sprigs of fresh thyme
- A small handful of fresh coriander
- coconut oil
- cooked rice (400g)
- pine nuts (40g)

METHOD

1. Heat 2 tablespoons of coconut oil in a frying pan on a medium heat. Add chopped garlic and onions and cook until translucent.

2. Next place pine nuts and mixed peppers chopped into small pieces into the pan with the tamarind paste, black pepper and chopped Scotch bonnet pepper.

3. Add the cooked rice to the pan and stir well. Finish by placing the butter, jerk paste and chopped coriander into the rice then give everything a good mix.

4. Fry on a high heat, stirring continuously for 3-4 minutes.

CREAMY MASHED POTATOES

It's all about the texture when it comes to mashed potatoes. This recipe delivers the creamy, silky, smooth mash we all love so keep this in mind when your hand begins to ache as you sieve your way to perfection.

INGREDIENTS

8 servings

2 tbsp dairy-free butter
coconut milk (200g)
large potatoes (Albert Bartlett work best) (1kg)
sea salt
black pepper
chives (optional)

METHOD

1 Peel the potatoes and chop roughly into small pieces.

2 Place in a saucepan of cold water, rinse and drain. Repeat 2-3 times until the water is clear.

3 Fill the saucepan with cold water, stopping just above the level of the potatoes and place on a high heat until the water comes to a boil. Reduce to a medium heat and boil until the potatoes are soft and fork tender.

4 Drain the potatoes into a colander then add them back to the dry saucepan. Put the pan on the heat and mix for 2-3 minutes to dry off any excess water.

5 In a separate saucepan, gently warm the butter and coconut milk.

6 Begin to mash the potatoes whilst slowly pouring in the hot butter and cream mixture. Use the masher to smash as many lumps as possible. For a completely smooth mash pass the potato through a fine mesh sieve.

7 Finally, add salt to taste and serve. I added an extra knob of butter plus chopped chives and coarse black pepper.

APPLE COBBLER

INGREDIENTS

6-8 servings

Filling

1 lemon, juiced and zested
1 tbsp cornstarch
2 tbsp cinnamon
1 tbsp coconut sugar
1 tbsp grated nutmeg
1 tsp ground ginger
2 tbsp orange extract
gala apples (600g)

Topping

2 cups spelt flour
2 to 3 tbsp coconut sugar
2 tsp baking powder
¾ cup coconut milk
pinch of salt
butter, cold (150g)

METHOD

1 Peel and slice the apples into a large bowl. Add the cinnamon, nutmeg, coconut sugar, ground ginger, orange extract and cornstarch. Massage the ingredients together then place in a large pie dish, ensuring the mixture is spread out evenly.

2 In a food processor, add the flour, salt, coconut sugar and baking powder then pulse together. Next, cut the cold butter into cubes, leave 4-6 cubes to one side to use later and pulse again until all the ingredients are mixed together.

3 Slowly pour the coconut milk into the mixture whilst continuing to pulse, until a crumbly wet consistency is formed.

4 Return to the pie dish and scatter the remaining cubes of butter across the top of the apples then spoon the topping mixture over the apples evenly. Don't worry if there are any gaps because the mixture will expand as it cooks.

5 Place the cobbler into the oven on 180°c (fan) for 40 minutes or until golden brown.

As an optional extra for added crunch you can add a dusting of finely crumbled ginger nut biscuits and lotus biscuits to the topping, 10 minutes before the cobbler is removed from the oven.

ACKEE & SWEET POTATO PIE

This recipe produces a pie with a diameter of 9cm. You will need: a pastry tin, ceramic baking beans (I use dried beans instead) and greaseproof paper.

INGREDIENTS

4 servings

1 onion
3 to 4 garlic cloves
1 small red pepper
1 spring onion
⅓ tsp jerk paste
1 tsp allspice
1 tsp thyme
1 tsp butter
1 tsp ground ginger
1 tbsp cinnamon
1 tsp allspice
1 tsp freshly grated nutmeg
1 tbsp ground flaxseed
1 tbsp dairy-free butter (80ml)
1½ tbsp spelt flour
ackee, tinned (180g)
black pepper
pinch of salt
coconut cream
ready-rolled shortcrust pastry
ceramic baking beans
sun-dried tomatoes
mushrooms (180g)
sweet potatoes (500g)

METHOD

1 Remove the ready-rolled pastry from the fridge at least 30 minutes before you are ready to begin. Unroll the pastry and drape it over your pastry tin. Gently push the pastry into the tin.

2 To blind bake the pastry, gently prod the base of the pastry with a fork. Scrunch up a large piece of greaseproof paper, big enough to stop above the inside of the pie tin so you can lift it out easily later.

Soak the paper in water to stop it burning in the oven, then squeeze it out and shake off any excess water. Place the wet greaseproof paper on top of your pastry then cover with the pie weights until the pastry tin is full. Cook in a preheated oven, on the lower shelf, for 30 minutes on 170°c (fan).

3 Put a tbsp of ground flaxseed into a small bowl with 2 1/2 tbsp water. Mix together and leave to stand for a few minutes until a gel-like consistency is formed.

Steam the sweet potatoes until fork tender, then mash them in a bowl with: ginger,

1 HOUR

cinnamon, allspice, nutmeg, a pinch of salt and the flaxseed mixture. Finally, stir in the melted butter and coconut cream then give all the ingredients a good mix.

4 Once the pie crust is finished blind baking, carefully remove the pie weights and greaseproof paper. If you used beans/chickpeas, store them in a jar to re-use when you next bake.

5 Spoon the sweet potato mixture evenly over the pastry, stopping just over halfway to the top of the tin. Place the pie back in the oven, on the lower shelf, for 45mins on 170°c (fan).

6 Place finely chopped onion and garlic in a frying pan with thinly diced red pepper plus the jerk paste, allspice, thyme and butter (or oil of your choice). Season with salt and pepper then leave to gently sauté for 10 minutes.

You may also choose to add the chopped mushrooms at this point however I prefer to cook them separately and add them to the mixture later.

Gently fold in the ackee and sundried tomatoes.

Spoon the ackee mixture over the sweet potato, return the pie to the oven for a final few minutes then garnish with fresh thyme and black pepper.

ACKEE & ARTICHOKES

INGREDIENTS

2 servings

1 onion
4 garlic cloves
½ red pepper
½ green pepper
1 spring onion
2 tomatoes
3 tbsp callaloo, tinned
1 tsp thyme
½ tsp coconut sugar
½ tsp Scotch bonnet pepper
⅓ tsp smoked paprika
1 tbsp coconut oil
smoky artichokes (200g)
ackee, tinned (200g)
sea salt
black pepper

METHOD

1 Cook finely chopped onions and garlic in a frying pan. Next place chopped peppers and spring onions into the pan with the coconut oil. Leave to sauté on a medium heat for 5 minutes.

2 Add chopped tomatoes to the mixture with the thyme, coconut sugar, Scotch bonnet pepper and smoked paprika. Season with salt and pepper then stir in the callaloo and smoky artichokes (I use ready-prepared ones).

Combine everything together for a further 5 minutes and slightly reduce the heat.

3 To finish, gently fold the ackee into the mixture. After a couple of minutes, turn off the heat and leave to rest with the lid on for a further 5 minutes before serving.

CASHEW CREAM CURRY

Cashew cream chickpea curry served with rice and gungo peas (pigeon peas), cinnamon-baked plantain, tomato and herb-spiced king oyster mushroom strips, sautéed cabbage and a black pepper and harissa topping.

INGREDIENTS

4 servings

- 1 cup cashew nuts
- 1 lemon, juiced
- 2 tbsp cumin seeds
- 1 onion
- 6 garlic cloves
- 3 large tomatoes
- 1 cinnamon stick
- 2 bay leaves
- 1 tbsp fresh thyme
- 1 Scotch bonnet pepper
- 2 tbsp Caribbean curry powder
- 1 tbsp coconut sugar
- coconut oil
- chickpeas, cooked (250g)
- sea salt
- black pepper

METHOD

1. Add the cashew nuts, water and lemon juice to a high speed blender and blitz until smooth to create the cashew cream.

2. Heat a little coconut oil in a frying pan. Place the chopped onions and garlic into the pan with the cumin then sauté for 3-4 minutes.

3. Pour chopped tomatoes into the pan with the bay leaves, thyme, Scotch bonnet pepper, curry powder, coconut sugar, cinnamon stick and a little water. Season with sea salt and black pepper then leave to cook for 5-7 minutes.

4. After 5-7 minutes, add the cashew cream, chickpeas and a little more water.

5. Cover the pan with a lid and cook on a low-medium heat for 20-25 minutes, stirring occasionally. Add more water during cooking if necessary.

GINGER & RUM COOKIES

INGREDIENTS

Makes 10 cookies

3 tbsp aquafaba
1 tsp baking powder
1 tsp cinnamon
1 tbsp ground ginger
1 tsp grated nutmeg
1 tsp lemon extract
2 tbsp cornflour
6 tbsp white spelt flour
dairy-free butter (100g)
brown sugar (80g)
Caribbean rum (optional)
fresh ginger (40g)

Aquafaba is the liquid from a can of chickpeas.

METHOD

1 Cut 100g of cold, dairy-free butter into cubes. Place the cubed butter and brown sugar into a food processor and pulse together until combined.

2 Place the butter mixture into a bowl with the aquafaba and stir together. Next add the baking powder, cinnamon, ground ginger, nutmeg and mix well.

3 Peel the fresh ginger then grate it into a bowl. Using a paper towel like a cheese cloth, place the grated ginger into a paper towel and squeeze all the juice into the butter mixture. Next put the lemon extract into the bowl with an optional splash of rum.

4 Stir the cornflour and spelt flour into the mixture. Cover the bowl and leave it in the fridge for at least 30 minutes (this will make the cookies easier to shape later).

5 Preheat the oven to 170°c (fan). Line a baking tray with greaseproof paper. Remove the dough from the fridge and work quickly to form into cookies. Break off a 30g piece of dough and roll into a ball. Press down into a cookie shape and place on the baking tray. Repeat until all the cookies are formed.

Remember the cookies will double in size, so leave plenty of space between each cookie. If

the dough becomes too wet at any point, pop it back into the fridge for a few minutes to firm up again.

6 Cook the cookies in the oven for 20-25 minutes until golden brown. Leave to cool for 15 minutes before eating.

BERBERE SPICED PLANTAIN

INGREDIENTS

1 large plantain
1 tbsp berbere spice mix
extra virgin olive oil

METHOD

1 Cut the plantain in half across its width then carefully slice each half lengthways into three.

2 Place the pieces of plantain in a mixing bowl and drizzle with olive oil.

3 Sprinkle the berbere spice over the plantain and mix together until all the pieces are evenly covered.

4 Heat extra virgin olive oil in a frying pan on a low-medium heat.

5 Carefully place the seasoned pieces of plantain into the pan and fry gently on each side until golden.

6 Remove from the heat and serve.

30 min - 45 min

RED LENTILS
in a red wine, Scotch bonnet & tomato sauce

Berbere spiced plantain with: red lentils in red wine, Scotch bonnet and tomato sauce, jollof rice and peas fusion, sautéed cabbage, jalapeno stuffed olives with sun-soaked tomatoes, hummus with black pepper and harissa and mac and cheese with toasted breadcrumbs.

INGREDIENTS

4 -6 servings

- 1 large onion
- 5 garlic cloves
- 1 red pepper
- 2 tbsp herbes de Provence
- 2 bay leaves
- 1 Scotch bonnet pepper
- 1 tbsp fresh thyme
- 1 tbsp coconut sugar
- passata (250g)
- coconut milk (150ml)
- red wine (150g)
- red lentils (250g)
- extra virgin olive oil

METHOD

1. Heat the oil in a pan on a medium heat. Add the chopped onions and garlic, diced red pepper, herbes de Provence, bay leaves, thyme and Scotch bonnet pepper (remove the seeds if you don't want it too spicy), stirring continuously for 4-5 minutes.

2. Pour the passata, coconut sugar, coconut milk and red wine into the mixture and cook for a further 5 minutes to allow the flavours to build.

3. Wash and rinse the red lentils in a fine strainer until the water runs clear then add to the pan, mixing everything together well.

4. Reduce the heat and place the lid on the pan, stirring occasionally.

5. Cook for 25-30 minutes until the lentils have softened, adding a little more water during cooking if necessary.

BUTTERED CABBAGE

INGREDIENTS

2 - 4 servings

1 pointed cabbage
2 tbsp dairy-free butter
sea salt
black pepper

METHOD

1 Heat the dairy-free butter in a saucepan.

2 Shred the cabbage into small ribbons and add them to the saucepan on the hob.

3 Season with sea salt and black pepper then cover with a lid.

4 Leave to cook on a low-medium heat for approximately 10 minutes until the cabbage is soft. Stir occasionally.

5 Once the cabbage is soft, remove from the heat and leave to cool for a few minutes before serving.

BBQ BURGERS

INGREDIENTS

Makes 6-8 burgers

5 garlic cloves
1 onion
1 tsp dried thyme
1 tbsp black pepper
1 tsp sea salt
½ Scotch bonnet pepper
1 tbsp dried jerk seasoning
2 tbsp barbecue sauce
plantain crisps (50g)
gram flour (100g)
a splash of rum (optional)
pumpkin or squash (100g)
mushrooms (240g)
dried couscous (50g)

METHOD

1 Peel and cut the pumpkin/squash into small cubes then boil in water or a steamer until soft. Once soft, drain away any excess water with a colander, then mash and leave to one side.

2 Heat a small amount of oil in a frying pan then add finely chopped onions and leave to sauté for 2-3 minutes. Next place diced garlic and scotch bonnet pepper into the pan and mix everything together. (For a lower level of spice, remove the seeds from the Scotch bonnet pepper before use).

3 Add finely chopped mushrooms to the onion mixture with the dried thyme. Stir in all the ingredients for 6-8 minutes on a medium heat until the excess water is almost gone. Remove from the heat and leave to cool.

4 Empty the couscous into a bowl then mix in the jerk seasoning. Pour 80ml of boiling water over the couscous so it is completely covered, then place a plate over the top and leave for 6 minutes.

1 HOUR

5 In a large bowl, mix together the mashed pumpkin/squash, mushroom mixture, cous-cous and barbecue sauce.

6 Put the plantain chips into a blender, blitz to a fine crumb then add to the mixture.

7 Sieve the gram flour into the mixture along with an optional splash of rum, adding extra flour if the mixture is too wet. The mixture should be dense enough to shape into burger patties without feeling overly sticky.

8 Roll out approx. 80g of the mixture into a ball and flatten into a burger shape. Repeat until all the burgers are made. Drizzle olive oil onto a baking tray lined with greaseproof paper and lay the burgers on it.

9 Cook in a preheated oven at 180°c for 15 minutes.

10 Finish the burgers on the barbecue grill. Drizzle the burgers with oil to stop them from sticking and baste the burgers with barbecue sauce on both sides whilst they cook on the grill. Cook for 2-3 minutes on each side.

If you are prepping your burgers in advance, after removing them from the oven at step 9, leave the burgers to cool then brush with barbecue sauce and store in the fridge for use later in the day. Allow time for the burgers to return to room temperature before cooking on the grill.

RGVEGAN

SPICED-UP BAKED BEANS

Spiced-up baked beans with: paprika and herb-roasted sweet potato, baked plantain with orange juice, hummus, sautéed tenderstem broccoli, gluten-free dumplings and sun-soaked tomatoes.

INGREDIENTS

2 - 4 servings

½ onion
2 garlic cloves
1 spring onion
½ red pepper
baked beans, tinned (300g)
black pepper
sea salt
hot pepper sauce

METHOD

1. Place chopped onions, garlic, red pepper and spring onions into a saucepan with a drizzle of extra virgin olive oil.

2. Season with sea salt and black pepper then leave the mixture to sauté on a medium heat for 4-5 minutes.

3. Stir in the baked beans and heat for a further 3-4 minutes until the sauce begins to bubble.

4. Turn off the heat and lightly season again with sea salt and black pepper.

5. Finish with a few drops of hot pepper sauce for an extra kick.

THE JEWELS

Chickpeas, sun-dried tomatoes & cashew nuts

This dish tastes great served hot or cold and can be eaten as either a side or main.

INGREDIENTS

2 - 4 servings

1 onion
5 garlic cloves
chickpeas (240g)
sundried tomatoes (100g)
cashew nuts (100g)
pumpkin seeds (30g)
capers (30g)
sea salt
black pepper
extra virgin olive oil

METHOD

1 Heat olive oil in a frying pan and add finely chopped onions and garlic. Season with a pinch of sea salt and black pepper then sauté for 5-6 minutes until the onions become translucent.

2 Add the chickpeas, chopped sun-dried tomatoes, cashew nuts, pumpkin seeds & capers to the pan. Mix together, adding a little more sea salt and black pepper to taste.

3 Turn off the heat and drizzle with extra virgin olive oil. Mix together and leave to cool a little before serving.

Served with quinoa, sautéed tenderstem brocolli, avocado, fried plantain and boiled pumpkin.

ACKEE & BUTTER BEAN CURRY

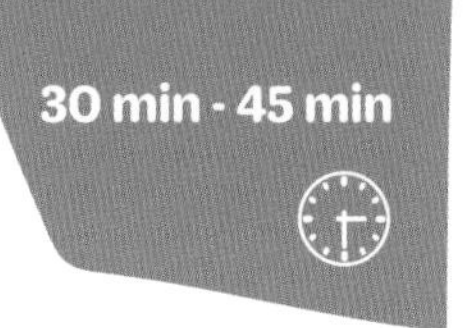

INGREDIENTS

4 servings

1 tsp cumin seeds
1 onion
5 garlic cloves
1 to 2 tsp fresh thyme
2 large tomatoes
½ tsp turmeric
2 tbsp curry powder
1 tsp cayenne pepper sea salt
2 to 3 sticks of lemon grass
1 lime, juiced
1 tbsp coconut sugar
fresh ginger (thumb-sized piece)
butter beans, cooked (230g)
king oyster mushrooms (200g)
ackee, tinned (230g)
black pepper
coconut oil

METHOD

1 Heat oil in a frying pan over a medium heat. Add chopped onions and garlic, cumin seeds, ginger and thyme.

2 Sauté for a couple of minutes before stirring in chopped tomatoes, turmeric, curry powder, cayenne pepper, sea salt and black pepper. Mix well.

3 Place the lemongrass on a chopping board and crush each stick under a knife before adding to the pan (this allows the flavours to be released during cooking).

4 Pour in the coconut milk, butter beans and coconut sugar. Stir all the ingredients together then reduce the heat and put the lid on the pan. Cook for 15 minutes, stirring occasionally.

5 Prepare the king oyster mushrooms by slicing across each mushroom to produce circular discs.

6 In a separate pan, heat some oil over a medium heat. Place the sliced mushroom, sea salt and black pepper into the pan, moving the pan continuously until the mushrooms begin to turn slightly golden. Add the cooked mushrooms to the curry and mix everything together.

7 Leave the curry to reduce for 10 minutes before gently folding in the ackee and lime juice.

FESTIVE ACKEE MIX

INGREDIENTS

4 servings

1 red onion
3 garlic cloves
1 apple (Royal Gala works best)
10 radishes (cherry tomato sized)
1 tbsp cinnamon
1 tbsp coconut sugar
10 cardamon pods
2 sprigs rosemary
sun-dried tomatoes chestnut mushrooms (100g)
ackee, tinned (340g)
splash of red wine (optional)
sea salt
black pepper

METHOD

1. Heat olive oil in a frying pan. Add finely chopped onions and garlic and season with a pinch of sea salt and black pepper. Sauté for 5-6 minutes until the onions become translucent.

2. Add chopped sun-dried tomatoes, apples and radishes followed by the cinnamon, coconut sugar, cardamon pods and rosemary. Mix together for 3-5 minutes, adding a little more sea salt, water or oil if necessary.

3. Place the rinsed and drained ackee along with the optional splash of wine to the pan. Leave to simmer for 5 minutes before turning off the heat.

4. Leave to cool for at least 10 minutes before serving for a fuller flavour.

Served with gluten free dumplings, chestnut mushrooms, green olives, hummus, avocado and tenderstem broccoli.

ACKEE IN CREAMY GARLIC SAUCE

INGREDIENTS

4 servings

1 onion
10 cherry tomatoes
½ red pepper
2 spring onions
1 tsp coconut sugar
7 garlic cloves
2 to 3 tbsp fresh parsley
coconut milk, tinned (150g)
sea salt
black pepper

METHOD

1 Heat olive oil in a frying pan and add finely chopped onions and garlic. Season with a pinch of sea salt and black pepper. Sauté for 5-6 minutes until the onions become translucent.

2 Add chopped cherry tomatoes and red pepper to the pan with the coconut sugar. Sauté on a low heat for 10 minutes.

3 Pour the mixture into a blender with the garlic, coconut cream and parsley. Blend until smooth.

4 Put the blended mixture back into the pan and stir well.

5 Gently stir in the rinsed and drained ackee then leave on a low heat for 5 minutes before turning off the heat completely. Leave to cool a little before serving.

Served with baked cho cho with cinnamon, fried plantain, fried breadfruit, chopped king oyster mushroom & mashed avocado.

PLANTAIN & MUSHROOM PITTA

Plantain and mushroom pitta with mint-coconut yoghurt, tomato salsa, avocado and lime.

INGREDIENTS

2 servings

1 plantain
2 king oyster mushrooms
1 red onion
1½ bell peppers
5 garlic cloves
1 tbsp cracked black pepper
1 tsp sea salt
½ tsp jerk paste
2 tbsp chargrilled red pepper paste
1 tbsp dried thyme
3 tbsp vegan coconut yoghurt
10 fresh mint leaves
1 lime, juiced
2 wholemeal pitta breads
sun-soaked tomatoes (150g)
olive oil, to drizzle

METHOD

1. Chop the plantain, king oyster mushrooms, red onion and peppers into chunky pieces that are all roughly the same size then place in a large bowl. I cut my plantain into circles approximately 0.5cm thick then slice each circle in half.

2. Add the finely chopped garlic cloves, sun-soaked tomatoes, black pepper, sea salt, olive oil, jerk paste, chargrilled red pepper paste and thyme to the bowl. Mix everything together well ensuring all the vegetables are evenly covered in the sauce.

3. Line a baking tray with greaseproof paper and spread the ingredients evenly across the tray. Roast in a preheated oven at 220°C for 15-20 minutes until the vegetables are slightly charred.

4. Toast the pitta breads and generously fill with the plantain and mushroom mixture.

5. Finely chop the mint leaves and mix with the coconut yoghurt and lime juice to create the mint- coconut dressing. Serve in a bowl alongside the stuffed pitta.

CHICKPEAS, JALAPEÑOS & OLIVES

Chickpeas, jalapeños and olives with pilau rice, steamed beetroot, hummus, plantain fritters and avocado.

INGREDIENTS

4 servings

2 jalapeños
8 to 10 cherry tomatoes
8 to 10 olives
½ onion
4 garlic cloves
1 lime, juiced
1 tsp cajun spice mix
chickpeas, tinned (240g)
tomato ketchup
sea salt
black pepper

METHOD

1 Drain and rinse the chickpeas.

2 Rub the chickpeas between your hands to remove as much of the outer skin as possible.

3 Heat oil in a frying pan then add chopped onions and crushed garlic. Sauté for 2-3 minutes until the onions become translucent.

4 Add the halved cherry tomatoes, jalapeños, sliced olives and chickpeas to the pan. Season the mixture with the cajun spice mix, a squirt of tomato ketchup, lime juice plus sea salt and black pepper to taste.

5 Mix the ingredients together well and sauté for a further 5-6 minutes, adding a little water if it starts to get dry.

6 Leave to cool a little before serving.

GLUTEN-FREE DUMPLINGS

Ackee mix with red wine rice, sautéed tenderstem broccoli, boiled cho cho (also known as chayote), shiitake mushroom, fried plantain, gluten - free dumplings and avocado.

INGREDIENTS

Makes 6-8 dumplings

5 tbsp gluten-free flour (Bob's Red Mill works best)
½ tsp of sea salt
1 tsp baking powder
2 tbsp psyllium husk
water (75-100ml)
dairy-free butter (40g)
coconut oil

METHOD

1 Place flour, baking powder and salt into a large bowl & mix together.

2 Add the butter and use your fingers to rub the butter into the flour to form a mixture that looks like fine crumble.

3 Mix the psyllium husk and water together in a cup. Leave to stand for a minute so the mixture solidifies then place it into the flour.

4 Use your hands to knead the ingredients until they start to form a smooth dough. The dough should be pliable enough to not stick to your hands - if it does, add a little more flour.

6 Lightly knead the dough into a circular shape and place it into a bowl/plate. Cover the bowl with damp kitchen towel and leave it in the fridge for 10 minutes.

7 Heat a frying pan on a medium heat with enough oil to cover the base. Remove the dough from the fridge. Tear off a small piece, roll it into a ball then flatten it in your hands to make a circular dumpling shape. Repeat for each dumpling.

8 Fry each dumpling on both sides for 3-5 minutes in the hot oil until golden.

RED WINE RICE

INGREDIENTS

4 servings

2 cups basmati rice
1 tbsp coconut sugar
½ tsp salt
coconut milk (100g)
100g red wine (100g)

METHOD

1 Add rice to a saucepan, fill with water then wash and drain. Repeat around 5 times until the water begins to become clear. Discard the water.

2 Pour water into the pan of rice to approximately 1cm above the rice and place on a high heat. Add the coconut milk, red wine, coconut sugar and salt. Gently mix the ingredients together using a fork - try to avoid over-stirring.

3 Once the rice begins to boil, give it a final stir, reduce the heat to low, top with a lid and leave to simmer.

4 After roughly 15 minutes, gently fluff the rice with a fork, starting from the bottom of the pan and turn off the heat. Put the lid back on and leave the steam to continue to cook the rice for a another 5 minutes.

FRIED BREADFRUIT

1 HOUR

Breadfruit has always been a family holiday favourite. Although perfectly delicious when cooked in other ways, the crisp, golden exterior of fried breadfruit is impossible to resist. Cooking times for breadfruit vary according to the size of the fruit. On average, a medium-sized breadfruit should take approximately 1 hour to cook in the oven. To check if your breadfruit is ready, pierce it with a knife. If the knife passes through the skin and flesh easily, the breadfruit is cooked.

1 Wash the skin.

2 Remove the stem.

3 Rub the skin with oil.

4 Cut a small cross into the base to allow air to escape.

5 Place in the oven at 200°C for 45 mins - 1 hour. Cook directly on the shelf, turning halfway through.

6 Cut in half and remove the heart.

7 Cut in half again then remove the core, seed and skin.

8 Cut into thick slices for frying.

9 Shallow fry each slice in oil for 2-3 minutes on each side until golden.

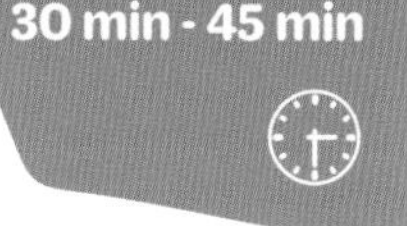

ACKEE & JACKFRUIT

Ackee and jackfruit in a tomato and scotch bonnet sauce with: quinoa and black-eyed beans, fried dumplings, cinnamon baked plantain, mushrooms and callaloo.

INGREDIENTS

4 servings

1 onion
6 garlic cloves
1 red pepper
2 tomatoes
1 tsp dried thyme
½ Scotch bonnet pepper, de-seeded
2 tbsp jerk bbq sauce
1 tbsp tomato puree
young jackfruit (400g)
ackee, tinned (340g)
small handful of parsley
sea salt
black pepper
extra virgin olive oil

METHOD

1 Chop all the vegetables and crush the garlic. Heat oil in a saucepan on a medium heat before adding onions and garlic. Season with sea salt and black pepper then cook for 5 minutes until the onions are translucent.

2 Add the red pepper, dried thyme and jackfruit to the pan, stirring everything together. Place the tomatoes, scotch bonnet, bbq sauce and tomato puree in a blender and blend till smooth.

3 Add the blended mixture to the pan and mix together well. Reduce on a low heat for 10-15 minutes, stirring frequently.

4 Rinse and drain the ackee then gently incorporate it into the mixture. Season again with sea salt and black pepper. Cook for a further 5 minutes before turning off the heat. Add chopped parsley and leave to cool a little before serving.

APPLE & ALMOND BUTTER OATS

INGREDIENTS

2 servings

1 cup oats
2 cups oat milk
2 tbsp cinnamon
1 tbsp nutmeg, grated
2 to 3 apples
almond butter
coconut oil

METHOD

1 Add oats, oat milk, cinnamon and nutmeg to a saucepan. Using a whisk, mix the ingredients together until the porridge begins to thicken.

2 Heat a little coconut oil in a frying pan on a medium heat. Add sliced apples to the pan, dust with cinnamon and fry for 5-6 minutes until golden.

3 Whisk more oat milk or water into the porridge until it reaches the desired consistency. Add to a bowl and top with the cooked apples plus a swirl of almond butter.

ACKEE-STUFFED DUMPLINGS

Ackee-stuffed dumpling with jerk-spiced sunflower seed mince, rice and peas, mac and cheese, buttered cabbage, fried plantain and avocado.

INGREDIENTS

4 serving

Ackee mix

2 onions
5 garlic cloves
1 spring onion
1 red pepper
1 Scotch bonnet pepper
1 tsp dried thyme
1 tbsp of coconut sugar
1 tbsp of tomato & herb seasoning (optional)
ackee, tinned (540g)
cracked black pepper
sea salt

Dumplings

1 tbsp coconut sugar
1 tsp cinnamon
1 tbsp dairy-free butter
6 to 7 tbsp vegan coconut yoghurt
self raising flour (250g)

METHOD

1 Warm oil in a pan on a medium heat then add chopped onions and crushed garlic. Season with sea salt and black pepper before sautéeing for 2-3 minutes until the onions become translucent.

2 Next place the spring onions (scallions), Scotch bonnet pepper, thyme, ackee, coconut sugar and seasoning into the pan. Gently mix the ingredients together and cook on a low to medium heat for about 10 minutes. Once done, set aside to cool.

3 Sieve the flour in a large bowl before adding the coconut sugar and cinnamon. Mix together then crumble in the dairy -free butter.

4 Stir in the coconut yoghurt, 2 tablespoons at a time then mix everything together until a smooth dough is formed. Knead the dough well before leaving it to rest in a bowl covered with damp kitchen paper for 10- 15 minutes.

5 Divide the dough into 6 pieces and roll out in circular shapes that are not too thin. Place 1½ tablespoons of the cooled ackee mixture into the centre of each dough circle. Gather up the edges of the first dough circle and press

together to seal the ackee inside then gently roll between your hands to form the familiar shape of a dumpling.

6 On a low - medium setting, heat a generous amount of oil in a frying pan. Ensure the oil is hot before adding 2-3 of the stuffed dumplings to the pan. Cook on each side for roughly 5 minutes until crisp and golden brown on the outside.

SUNFLOWER SEED MINCE BOLOGNESE

with ackee

Sunflower seed mince bolognese with ackee, cajun-spiced sweet potato wedges, fried plantain, buttered cabbage, mashed avocado and boiled cho cho.

INGREDIENTS

4 - 6 servings

2 onions
8 garlic cloves
2 tbsp herbes de Provence (or Italian herbs)
1 tbsp dried rosemary
1 red pepper
1 green pepper
1 courgette
3 large tomatoes
½ de-seeded Scotch bonnet pepper
4 sprigs of fresh rosemary
tomato passata (500g)
red wine (optional) (100ml)
sunflower seed mince (100g)
ackee, tinned (340g)
sea salt
black pepper

METHOD

1. Dice all the vegetables and crush the garlic for an even cook. Heat oil in a saucepan on a medium heat. Add the onions and garlic, season with sea salt and black pepper then cook for 5 minutes until the onions are translucent.

2. Stir in the red and green peppers followed by the courgette, tomatoes and Scotch bonnet pepper. Add the herbes de Provence and dried rosemary before giving the mixture a good stir. Cook for 5-7 minutes, stirring frequently.

3. Add the sunflower seed mince to the sauce. Next pour in the optional red wine plus the tomato passata and fresh rosemary. Stir everything together, seasoning again with sea salt and black pepper.

4. Add a cup of water to the mixture, top with a lid and cook for 25 minutes on a low heat, stirring frequently.

5. Rinse and drain the ackee then gently stir it into the bolognese. Cook for a further 5 minutes before turning off the heat and leaving it to cool a little in the pan before serving.

FRENCH TOAST

INGREDIENTS

6 servings

4 tbsp chickpea flour
½ tbsp baking powder
2 tbsp ground cinnamon
½ cup aquafaba
1 small ripe plantain, mashed
1 cup coconut milk
1 to 2 tbsp coconut sugar
1 tbsp vanilla bean extract
¼ cup extra virgin olive oil
6 slices of bread

METHOD

1 Using an electric whisk, whisk the aquafaba until it has a foamy white consistency.

2 In a separate large bowl, mix together the chickpea flour, baking powder, ground cinnamon and coconut sugar.

3 Next add the mashed plantain, coconut milk, vanilla bean extract and extra virgin olive oil. Stir everything together then fold in the whisked aquafaba.

4 Heat a little oil in a frying pan/griddle pan. Immerse a slice of bread in the batter then fry on each side for 1-2 minutes until golden. Repeat for each slice of bread.

JERK KING OYSTER MUSHROOMS

Jerk king oyster mushrooms with rice and peas, mac and cheese, mashed avocado, fried plantain, fried dumplings and charred tomato

INGREDIENTS

2 servings

1 tsp jerk paste
1 tsp of dried thyme
5 tbsp jerk BBQ sauce
king oyster mushrooms (200g)
extra virgin olive oil
sea salt

METHOD

1. Slice the king oyster mushrooms lengt ways and place in a mixing bowl.

2. Pour the jerk paste, jerk BBQ sauce, dried thyme, sea salt and a generous drizzle of extra virgin oil over the mushrooms.

3. Gently mix the ingredients together until the mushrooms are evenly covered.

4. Line a baking tray with greaseproof paper and spread the marinated mushrooms evenly across it.

5. Place into a preheated oven at 180°c for 15 minutes until 'fork tender'.

JAMAICAN CALLALOO

INGREDIENTS

2 - 4 servings

1 onion
4 garlic cloves
3 spring onions
1 large tomato
½ Scotch bonnet pepper
3 sprigs of thyme
callaloo, tinned (540g)
sea salt
black pepper

METHOD

1 Wash and drain the callaloo and leave to one side.

2 Drizzle some oil into a large saucepan and heat until warm. Add chopped onions, garlic and spring onions to the pan. Sauté for 3-4 minutes.

3 Place chopped tomatoes, the Scotch bonnet pepper and thyme into the pan and mix everything together for a further 3-4 minutes.

4 Add the drained callaloo, season with salt and pepper then mix well.

5 Leave on a low heat and continue to cook for 7-8 minutes.

ESME'S MAC & CHEESE

One of my favourite versions of a vegan mac & cheese by Esme Carr with little addtion of plantain crisps.

INGREDIENTS

4 - 6 servings

- ½ onion
- 2 garlic cloves
- 1 tsp dried thyme
- ⅕ tsp smoked paprika
- ⅕ tsp hot chilli powder
- 1 tbsp tomato ketchup
- 2 tbsp dairy free butter
- 3 tbsp plain flour
- 4 to 6 tbsp panko breadcrumbs
- oat milk (400ml)
- grated vegan cheese (150g)
- penne pasta (300g)
- sweet plantain crisps, crushed (85g)

METHOD

1. Heat oil in a saucepan on a medium heat then add chopped onions, garlic, dried thyme, smoked paprika and hot chilli powder. Sauté for 2-3 minutes before adding a squirt of tomato ketchup.

2. Add the butter to the pan, followed by the flour once the butter has melted. Stir the mixture for 2-3 minutes to ensure the flour is cooked out. It will look a little doughy by the end.

3. Pour the milk into the mixture and whisk until it has the consistency of a sauce. Add the vegan cheese into the sauce and whisk until the cheese has melted.

4. Put some water in a pan to boil. Add the pasta and a little sea salt. When the pasta is cooked, drain the water and stir in the sauce until all the pasta is fully covered.

5. Pour the mixture into a baking dish and top with crushed plantain crisps and panko breadcrumbs. Cook at 200°C for 15 minutes in a preheated oven until the topping is golden brown.

PLANTAIN LASAGNE

INGREDIENTS

2-4 servings

1 large onion
8 garlic cloves
4 tbsp herbes de Provence
5 red peppers
½ cup red lentils
1 Scotch bonnet pepper
2 plantains
2 tbsp extra virgin olive oil
1 lemon
8 pasta sheets
2 to 3 tbsp pine nuts, toasted (optional)
chopped tomatoes, tinned (800g)
red wine (100ml)
vegetable stock (100ml)
ackee, tinned (200g)
cashew nuts (100g)
coconut milk (200ml)
sea salt
black pepper

METHOD

1 Heat the oil in a deep saucepan on a medium heat. Add chopped onions, crushed garlic, herbes de Provence, sea salt and black pepper. Sauté until the onions turn translucent.

2 Finely chop the red pepper and add it to the pan. Stir for 1-2 minutes then mix in the tomatoes, red wine and vegetable stock. Leave to cook on a low heat.

3 Rinse the lentils 2-3 times until the water is clear. Stir the lentils into the sauce and give everything a good mix. Pierce a hole in the scotch bonnet pepper and add it to the pan, seasoning everything again with salt and pepper.

4 Reduce the heat to a low setting, pop the lid on the pan and leave the sauce to cook for a further 30-35 minutes, stirring occasionally. In the final 5 minutes, when the lentils are soft, stir in the ackee.

5 Chop the plantain in half along the width then cut each half lengthways into slices roughly 0.5cm thick. Fry each slice in oil on both sides until golden.

6 Place the cashew nuts, coconut milk, lemon juice, extra virgin olive oil, sea salt and black pepper in a blender and blend until smooth. Gradually add water to the mixture until you're left with a sauce with a creamy consistency.

7 Heat a large saucepan of water and bring to a boil. Place the pasta sheets into the boiling water, sprinkle with sea salt and cook for 3-4 minutes. Do not cook more than 4 pasta sheets at a time because they will end up sticking together.

Stir the water from time to time to keep the sheets apart. When the time is up, remove the sheets from the water and leave them spread out on a plate.

8 Place each layer of the lasagne into a deep baking dish in the following order: pasta sheets, lentil sauce, fried plantain then cashew sauce. Repeat until you reach the top of the dish. Cook the lasagne in a pre-heated oven at 180°c for 15-20 minutes. Leave to cool a little before serving.

Serve topped with chopped parsley, basil and toasted pine nuts.

PLANTAIN & SWEET POTATO PURÉE & APPLE PURÉE

Packed with flavour and nutrients, these were my nephew's favourite purees when he was little.

Photographed by Ramoan

PLANTAIN & SWEET POTATO PURÉE

Steam half a ripe plantain with half a sweet potato until soft then blend with a little cinnamon until smooth.

APPLE PURÉE

Place chopped apples into a saucepan with a little water, cinnamon and 2-3 cloves. Cook until soft then blend till smooth.

CASHEW & COCONUT CREAM PENNE

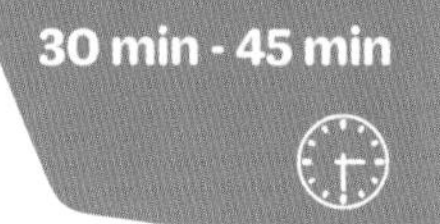

INGREDIENTS

2 servings

1 onion
5 garlic cloves
½ red pepper
½ cup cashew nuts
1 cup coconut milk
¼ cup olive oil
1 lime
1 tbsp herbes de provence
buckwheat penne (150g)
chickpeas (tinned) (240g)
parsley
sea salt
black pepper

METHOD

1 Drain, rinse and dry the chickpeas then place them in a baking tray. Sprinkle the chick-peas with olive oil followed by the herbes de provence, salt and pepper. Massage the seasoning into the chickpeas and cook in a preheated oven on 200oc for 10 minutes.

2 Heat a frying pan with a little oil on a low - medium heat and place in finely chopped onion. Sauté for a few minutes until onions become translucent and then add x4 finely chopped garlic cloves, thin strips of red pep-per, salt & pepper.

3 Heat a saucepan with water and a pinch of salt for your pasta. Cook for a 1-2 minutes un-der the pastas recommended cooking time.

4 To a blender add cashew nuts, coconut milk, garlic clove, juice of a lime and a drizzle of olive oil. Blend until smooth gradually adding water until a pourable creamy consistency is formed.

5 Add the oven baked chickpeas (leaving a small amount to the side for topping later) to the frying pan of onion and garlic followed by the coconut cashew cream. Mix together and reduce to a low heat.

Then add the cooked and drained pasta. The sauce may begin to thicken to which you

can gradually add some of the pasta water to return it back to a wetter consistency.

Combine together and cook on a low heat for 2-3 minutes.

6 Finely chop some fresh parsley and mix it into the mixture. Served and top with some more fresh parsley, the roasted chickpeas and black pepper to taste.

TISH'S NON-BASIC SALAD

Inspired by Tish Wonders 'Non Basic Salad Recipe' this is my take on creating a filling and colourful salad packed with an ultimate flavour combination. This is one you can allow your creativity to flow and use ingredients you love to create your own version.

WHAT I USED

Pea shoots
Watercress
Radicchio
Sweet potato
Beetroot
Red onion
Kalamata olives
Tomatoes
Chickpeas
Kimchi
Avocado
Pumpkin seeds
Pine nuts
Cress
Tender-stem broccoli
Plantain
Extra virgin olive oil
Tamari
Sea salt
Black pepper

SWEET POTATO

Dice your washed and peeled sweet potato (if preferred) and place in a lined oven tray. Drizzle with olive oil and season with salt and pepper. Place in a pre-heated oven at 190°c for 15 minutes or until potatoes are soft.

CHICKPEAS

Place washed, drained and dried chickpeas into a bowl and add ½ a teaspoon of garlic powder, paprika, herbes de provence, a drizzle of olive oil plus sea salt & pepper to taste. Mix together and place on a lined baking tray. Place in the oven at 190°c for 10-15 minutes until crispy and golden.

TENDER-STEM BROCCOLI

Wash and dry the broccoli and massage with a drizzle of olive oil. Place in a baking tray and put in the oven at 190°c for 5-10 minutes until lightly charred,

FRIED PLANTAIN

Directions on page 15.

PINE NUTS

Gently toast the pine nuts in a heated frying pan until colour is shown.

PUMPKIN SEEDS

Add the pumpkin seeds to a lined baking tray and bake for 10 minutes at 190°c. Splash with Tamari once complete.

BEETROOT

Wash and peel beetroot. Cut into cubes and place into a steamer until soft.

DRESSING

¼ cup extra virgin olive oil
1 tbsp lemon juice
½ tsp dijon mustard
ginger (grated), (1cm)
drizzle of maple syrup
Sea salt
Black pepper
A small handful of fresh parsley (chopped)

Place all ingredients into a bowl and whisk together.

HOW TO ASSEMBLE

Begin with a base of pea shoots and watercress and layer, radicchio, sweet potato, beetroot, red onion, kalamata olives, roasted chick peas, tomatoes, roasted tender-stem broccoli, roasted chickpeas, kimchi, avocado, and fried plantain. Top with pumpkin seeds, toasted pine nuts, cress, and the dressing.

ACKNOWLEDGEMENTS

A massive thank you to my Nanny who has showed me the ropes on the traditional cooking of some of Jamaica's cuisine. This has allowed me to adapt according where necessary and allow flavour to be the forefront of my food. You've allowed me to use your kitchen space for all of my needs over the years, from doing meal preparations, recipe testing and content creation. You are always at hand to help whenever needed making this journey that much easier and I am truly grateful.

My sister Francesca, you helped so much with deliveries; driving all over London for hours so food could be delivered safely. That first, last minute delivery trip to Birmingham was officially where this begun (and where it could have ended if I had continued to drive lol).

You taste tested and gave your approval too many dishes which gave me the confidence to put it out and make it available to others. Thank you so much.

Mum, thank you for your beautiful words of encouragement over the years and fully supporting everything I do. You are one of the driving forces for me to keep pushing and growing. Thank you for your assistance with deliveries and your countless offers of help. I wouldn't be here without you... literally.

Dad, thank you for your encouragement and support over the years. You showed me the definition of hard work. I've seen you work everyday of my life with very little break because you have a genuine love for what you do. I aspired to do the same.

Tish, you have been my biggest inspiration when it comes to the art of food. Your natural artistry, precision and knowledge on the subject has taught me so much. Thank you for your constant words of encouragement, sharing your techniques, ideas and enhancing my creativity. YDELM x

To everyone who has shown love and support over the years it doesn't go unnoticed. Thank you for allowing me to do what do.

I love you all.

Photographed by Ramoan